AQA
Level 2

Certificate in
Further
Mathematics
EXAM PRACTICE

Authors
Val Hanrahan,
Andrew Ginty

Series editor
Alan Walton

HODDER
EDUCATION
AN HACHETTE UK COMPANY

Every effort has been made to trace all copyright holders, but if any have been inadvertently overlooked, the Publishers will be pleased to make the necessary arrangements at the first opportunity.

Although every effort has been made to ensure that website addresses are correct at time of going to press, Hodder Education cannot be held responsible for the content of any website mentioned in this book. It is sometimes possible to find a relocated web page by typing in the address of the home page for a website in the URL window of your browser.

Hachette UK's policy is to use papers that are natural, renewable and recyclable products and made from wood grown in well-managed forests and other controlled sources. The logging and manufacturing processes are expected to conform to the environmental regulations of the country of origin.

Orders: please contact Bookpoint Ltd, 130 Park Drive, Milton Park, Abingdon, Oxon OX14 4SE. Telephone: +44 (0)1235 827827. Fax: +44 (0)1235 400401. Email education@bookpoint.co.uk Lines are open from 9 a.m. to 5 p.m., Monday to Saturday, with a 24-hour message answering service. You can also order through our website: www.hoddereducation.co.uk

ISBN: 978 1 5104 6076 8
© Andrew Ginty and Val Hanrahan 2020
First published in 2020 by
Hodder Education,
An Hachette UK Company
Carmelite House
50 Victoria Embankment
London EC4Y 0DZ
www.hoddereducation.co.uk
Impression number   10 9 8 7 6 5 4 3 2 1
Year   2024 2023 2022 2021 2020

Cover photo © Satit_Srihin/stock,adobe.com

Typeset in Bembo Std 11/13.2pt by Aptara, Inc.

Printed in the UK by CPI Group

A catalogue record for this title is available from the British Library.

MIX
Paper from
responsible sources
FSC™ C104740
FSC
www.fsc.org

Contents

**Full worked solutions are available at
www.hoddereducation.co.uk/AQAL2MathsExamPractice**

Introduction

This book has been written to supplement the AQA Level 2 Certificate in Further Mathematics textbook, but it could also be used to provide additional exercises for anyone studying Mathematics beyond GCSE. There are over 350 questions to support successful preparation for the specification released by AQA for first assessment in 2019.

Grouped according to topic, the chapters follow the content of the AQA Level 2 Certificate in Further Mathematics textbook.

Each chapter starts with short questions to support retrieval of content and straightforward application of skills learned during the course. The demand gradually builds through each exercise, with the later questions requiring significant mathematical thinking and, often, problem solving strategies. This reflects the range of styles of question that will be found in the exam.

Answers are provided in this book, and full worked solutions and mark allocations to all questions can be found online at **www.hoddereducation.co.uk/AQAL2MathsExamPractice**

1 Number and algebra I

Exercise 1.1 Numbers and the number system

1 Calculate 3.7% of 54 kg.

2 Increase £17 by 36%.

3 **(i)** Write the ratio $4.14 : 2.7$ in the form $a : b$ where a and b are integers.

   (ii) Write your answer to part (i) in the form $1 : \dfrac{m}{n}$ where m and n are integers.

4 Write the ratio $4\dfrac{1}{6} : 1\dfrac{1}{4}$ in the form $p : q$ where p and q are integers.

5 Decrease £23.59 by 5.6%.

6 Without using a calculator, evaluate $\dfrac{3}{4} - \dfrac{2}{5} \div \dfrac{7}{8}$.

7 In a test, the ratio of passes to fails is $13 : 5$.

   (i) Write the number of passes as a fraction of the total tests taken.

   (ii) Hence work out the percentage of passes to 1 decimal place.

8 Linda and Alan fire the **same** number of arrows at a target.
   Linda's ratio of hits to misses is $5 : 1$.

   Alan's ratio of hits to misses is $3 : 2$.

   (i) Write down Alan's hit rate as a percentage of the total number of arrows he fired.

PS **(ii)** Work out the least possible difference between their numbers of hits.

Exercise 1.2 Simplifying expressions

1 Simplify each of these expressions.

   (i) $x(x + 2y) - x(y - x)$

   (ii) $2p(3p - 4q) - 7q(p + 5q)$

2 Factorise each of these expressions.

   (i) $x^2y - xy^2$

   (ii) $8p^3q^2 - 6pq^5$

3 Simplify and factorise each of these expressions.

   (i) $a(a + 6) - a(4 - a)$

   (ii) $p(p + q) - p(3 + q) + 7p$

4 Simplify each of these expressions.

   (i) $2a^2b \times 3ab^3$

   (ii) $3x^3y \times 2xy^3 \times 5y^2z$

5 Simplify each of these expressions.

   (i) $\dfrac{6m^2n}{8m^3n^4}$

   (ii) $\dfrac{5xy}{8x^3} \div \dfrac{25x^4y^2}{6xy^3}$

6 Write each of these as a single simplified fraction.

(i) $\dfrac{2}{p} + \dfrac{5}{q}$

(ii) $\dfrac{x}{3} + \dfrac{2}{x} - \dfrac{5}{3x}$

7 Simplify $\dfrac{x}{y} + \dfrac{2x}{3} \times \dfrac{5}{y}$.

PS 8 The angles of the octagon are all 90° and 270°.

Its side lengths are given in terms of p.

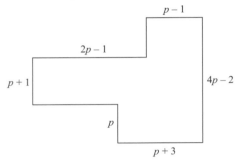

(i) Work out its perimeter in terms of p.

(ii) Work out its area in terms of p.

Exercise 1.3 Solving linear equations

1 Solve these equations.

(i) $2x + 5 = x - 3$

(ii) $5y - 3 = 3y + 7$

2 Solve these equations.

(i) $3(2x - 4) = x + 7$

(ii) $4(5x + 3) = 3(2x - 7) - 2$

3 The three angles of a triangle are $(2x - 5)°$, $(x - 11)°$ and $4x°$.

(i) Work out the size of the smallest angle.

(ii) What type of triangle is it?

4 Solve $\dfrac{p}{2} + \dfrac{p}{3} = 7$.

5 The length of a rectangular field is 20 m greater than its width, and its perimeter is 320 m.

(i) Write an equation in terms of w, its width.

(ii) Hence, work out the area of the field.

6 Solve $\dfrac{x+3}{2} + \dfrac{2x-5}{4} = 7$.

7 (i) Write down the lowest common multiple of 3, 5 and 4.

(ii) Solve $\dfrac{x+2}{3} + \dfrac{x}{5} - \dfrac{3x}{4} = 7$.

PS 8 The sum of four consecutive even numbers is 156.

Work out the smallest of the four even numbers.

Exercise 1.4 Algebra and number

1 30% of m is the same as 80% of n.

   (i) Write an equation linking m and n.

   (ii) Write n as a percentage of m.

2 24 increased by a% is the same as b decreased by 24%.

   (i) Write an equation linking a and b.

   (ii) Hence show that $19b - 6a = k$, where k is an integer to be found.

PS **3** Approximately 12% of the population are left-handed, and twice as many men are left-handed as women. Also, approximately 50% of the population are men, and 50% are women.

   In a group of 60 men and 25 women, estimate the number of left-handed people.

PS **4** The ratio of boys to girls in a room is $5 : 2$.

   15 boys leave the room and 4 girls enter.

   The ratio of boys to girls is now $10 : 9$.

   How many boys are now in the room?

5 The length of a rectangle is increased by 25%, and the width reduced by x%. The area of the rectangle remains the same.

   Work out the value of x.

6 The original price of a handbag is £h.
The original price is reduced by 20%.

   (i) Write down the new price in terms of h.

   The new price is then increased by 50% to give a final price.

   (ii) Write down the ratio of the original price to the final price in the form $a : b$, where a and b are integers.

   The final price is £35 more than the original price.

   (iii) Work out the original price.

7 $x : y = 3 : 5$

   (i) Work out the ratio $2x - y : 3x + y$.

      Write your answer in the form $a : b$, where a and b are integers.

   $y : z = 7 : 2$

   (ii) Write z as a percentage of x, correct to 1 decimal place.

PS **8** m is 20% greater than n.
$p : n = 6 : 7$

   Write p as a percentage of m correct to 1 decimal place.

Exercise 1.5 Expanding brackets

1 Expand and simplify each of these expressions.

   (i) $(x + 1)(x + 2)$

   (ii) $(2x + 5)(x - 3)$

2 Expand and simplify each of these expressions.

   (i) $(m + 1)(m^2 - m + 1)$

   (ii) $(x - 1)(x^4 + x^3 + x^2 + x + 1)$

3 Expand and simplify each of these expressions.

(i) $(x + 3)(x - 1)(x + 1)$

(ii) $(2y - 3)(3y + 1)(y - 5)$

4 Simplify each of these expressions.

(i) $(x + 3)(x - 4) - (x + 2)(x - 1)$

(ii) $(2m + 3)(m - 5) - (m + 4)(m - 3)$

5 Given that $(x^2 - 3x + a)(x^2 + bx - 1) \equiv x^4 - 2x^3 + 7x - 4$, work out the values of a and b.

6 (i) Expand and simplify $(3m - 1)^2$.

(ii) Hence work out the simplified expansion of $(3m - 1)^3$.

7 (i) Expand and simplify each of these expressions.

(a) $(x^3 - 2)(x^2 + 5)$

(b) $(3 + x^3)(x - 7)$

(ii) Hence expand and simplify $(x^3 - 2)(x^2 + 5) - (3 + x^3)(x - 7)$.

8 The dimensions of a cuboid are $(x + 1)$, $(x - 2)$ and $(2x + 1)$.

(i) Write the volume in terms of x.

(ii) Write the surface area in terms of x.

Give your answers in expanded and simplified form.

Exercise 1.6 Binomial expansions – using Pascal's triangle only

1 Expand and simplify $(x + 2)^3$.

2 Express $(2x + y)^4$ as a sum of five simplified terms.

3 (i) Write down the simplified expansion of $(a + b)^5$.

(ii) Hence work out the simplified expansion of $(2x - 3y)^5$.

4 The first three numbers in the 12th row of Pascal's triangle are $1, 12, 66$.

(i) Write down the first three numbers in the 13th row of Pascal's triangle.

(ii) Hence write down the first three terms, in ascending powers of x, of the expansion of $(2 + x)^{13}$.

5 Work out the coefficient of the x^2 term in the expansion of $(2x + 3)^6$.

PS 6 The first four numbers in the 7th row of Pascal's triangle are $1, 7, 21, 35$.

Work out the coefficient of x^2 in the expansion of $\left(x^2 + \dfrac{2}{x} \right)^7$.

PS 7 The simplified expansion of $(ax + y)^n$ includes the term $80x^3y^2$.

(i) Write down the value of n.

(ii) Hence work out the value of a.

(iii) Hence work out the coefficient of the x^2y^3 term.

PS 8 The first six numbers in the 10th row of Pascal's triangle are $1, 10, 45, 120, 210, 252$.

Work out the constant term in the expansion of $\left(3x - \dfrac{2}{x} \right)^{10}$.

Exercise 1.7 Surds: simplifying expressions containing square roots

Do not use a calculator for this exercise.

1 **(i)** Simplify $\sqrt{72}$ and $\sqrt{50}$.

   (ii) Hence simplify $\sqrt{72} + \sqrt{50}$.

   (iii) Hence write $\sqrt{72} + \sqrt{50}$ in the form $\sqrt{a}$.

2 Simplify the following by rationalising their denominators.

   (i) $\dfrac{1}{\sqrt{2}}$ **(ii)** $\dfrac{6}{\sqrt{2}}$ **(iii)** $\dfrac{5}{\sqrt{3}}$

   (iv) $\dfrac{\sqrt{7}}{\sqrt{2}}$ **(v)** $\dfrac{6}{2\sqrt{3}}$ **(vi)** $\sqrt{\dfrac{8}{5}}$

3 Write $\dfrac{3}{\sqrt{2}} + \dfrac{5}{\sqrt{8}}$ as a single rationalised fraction.

4 Solve $x\sqrt{32} + 2x\sqrt{2} = \sqrt{98}$.

5 Simplify each of these numerical expressions to the form $a + \sqrt{b}$ $\left(\text{or } a - \sqrt{b}\right)$, where a and b are rational numbers.

   (i) $\dfrac{1}{\sqrt{2}-1} + \dfrac{1}{\sqrt{2}+1}$ **(ii)** $\dfrac{3}{2+\sqrt{3}} + \dfrac{1}{2-\sqrt{3}}$

   (iii) $\dfrac{7}{\sqrt{8}-2} - \dfrac{3}{\sqrt{8}+2}$ **(iv)** $\dfrac{5}{4-\sqrt{2}} - \dfrac{3}{4+\sqrt{2}}$

6 A rectangle has length $\left(4 + \sqrt{2}\right)$ cm and width $\left(4 - \sqrt{2}\right)$ cm.

   (i) Write down its perimeter.

   (ii) Work out the area of the rectangle.

   (iii) Calculate the length of one of its diagonals.

7 **(i)** Expand and simplify $(a + b)^4$.

   (ii) Hence expand and simplify $\left(3 + \sqrt{2}\right)^4$.

8 Solve the following equations.

   (i) $\dfrac{3x}{\sqrt{2}} + \dfrac{1}{\sqrt{2}} = \sqrt{8}$ **(ii)** $\dfrac{2w}{\sqrt{3}} - \dfrac{1}{\sqrt{12}} = 5$

   (iii) $\dfrac{5y}{\sqrt{8}} = \sqrt{18} + \dfrac{y}{\sqrt{2}}$ **(iv)** $2\left(\dfrac{7}{\sqrt{20}} - \dfrac{m}{\sqrt{5}}\right) = \dfrac{1}{\sqrt{45}} + \dfrac{2m}{\sqrt{80}}$

9 Solve $(\sqrt{3} - x)^3 = 9\sqrt{3} - x(9 + x^2)$.

Exercise 1.8 Surds: rationalising denominators with two terms

Do not use a calculator for this exercise.

1 Rationalise the denominators of these fractions.

   (i) $\dfrac{2}{\sqrt{2}-1}$ **(ii)** $\dfrac{5}{7+\sqrt{3}}$ **(iii)** $\dfrac{\sqrt{5}}{3+\sqrt{5}}$ **(iv)** $\dfrac{2\sqrt{6}}{5-\sqrt{6}}$

   (v) $\dfrac{\sqrt{7}}{9-2\sqrt{7}}$ **(vi)** $\dfrac{3+\sqrt{2}}{3-\sqrt{2}}$ **(vii)** $\dfrac{5-\sqrt{3}}{4+\sqrt{3}}$ **(viii)** $\dfrac{6+2\sqrt{10}}{3\sqrt{10}-7}$

2 Write each fraction in the form $a + b\sqrt{2}$, where a and b are rational numbers.

(i) $\dfrac{\sqrt{2}}{5-\sqrt{2}}$

(ii) $\dfrac{7+\sqrt{2}}{7-\sqrt{2}}$

(iii) $\dfrac{6+\sqrt{2}}{\sqrt{2}-1}$

(iv) $\dfrac{5-\sqrt{8}}{\sqrt{18}+4}$

3 Write each fraction in the form $a + \sqrt{b}$, where a and b are rational numbers.

(i) $\dfrac{2}{\sqrt{3}-1}$

(ii) $\dfrac{5}{\sqrt{2}-1}$

(iii) $\dfrac{3}{6-\sqrt{3}}$

(iv) $\dfrac{2+\sqrt{5}}{4-\sqrt{5}}$

4 (i) Expand $(\sqrt{5}-\sqrt{2})(\sqrt{5}+\sqrt{2})$.

(ii) Hence rationalise the denominator of $\dfrac{\sqrt{5}+\sqrt{2}}{\sqrt{5}-\sqrt{2}}$.

5 A rectangle has a width of $(5-\sqrt{2})$ cm and an area of $(18+\sqrt{2})$ cm². Work out its length.

6 The area of a trapezium is $(50 + \sqrt{162})$ cm².

The trapezium has two parallel sides of lengths $(7+\sqrt{8})$ cm and $(6-\sqrt{18})$ cm.

(i) Work out the sum of the two parallel side lengths.

(ii) Hence calculate the perpendicular distance between the parallel sides.

7 (i) Expand and simplify $(\sqrt{3}+\sqrt{2}-1)(\sqrt{3}-\sqrt{2}+1)$.

(ii) Hence rationalise the denominator of $\dfrac{5-\sqrt{2}}{\sqrt{3}+\sqrt{2}-1}$.

(iii) Rationalise the denominator of $\dfrac{3}{\sqrt{5}-\sqrt{3}+2}$.

8 Rationalise the denominator of $\dfrac{\sqrt{5}+\sqrt{2}-3}{\sqrt{5}-\sqrt{2}+1}$.

Exercise 1.9 The product rule for counting

1 Work out the number of arrangements of the letters LMNOPQ.

2 The digits 3, 5, 2, 7 are arranged to form a four-digit number.

(i) How many different four-digit multiples of 5 can be formed?

(ii) How many different four-digit numbers, which are not multiples of 5, can be formed?

3 A four-digit code is to be chosen using the digits 0 to 9.
0 may be chosen as the first digit.

(i) If digits can be repeated, how many different codes can be chosen?

(ii) If no digit can be repeated, how many codes can be chosen?

PS 4 The diagram shows all routes from A to B.

Following the arrows, how many different routes from A to B are possible?

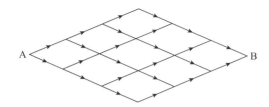

PS 5 Eight different books are lined up on a shelf.

(i) How many different arrangements are possible?

Two more books are added.

The two new books are identical to each other but are not the same as any of the original eight books. Swapping these two books does not give a different arrangement.

(ii) How many different arrangements of the ten books are possible?

6 (i) How many numbers between 40 000 and 100 000 include the digit 3 exactly once?

(ii) How many numbers between 40 000 and 100 000 include the digit 3 at least once?

PS 7 A group of letters is palindromic if the arrangement reads the same backwards as forwards, e.g. BFPFB is palindromic.
Seven cards are shown here.

How many different palindromic arrangements are possible if

(i) all seven cards must be used

(ii) exactly four of the seven cards must be used

(iii) at least two of the cards must be used?

PS 8 Here are eight digits: 1 2 3 4 5 6 7 8

(i) If each digit can appear no more than once, how many different five-digit numbers can be formed?

(ii) If each digit can appear any number of times, how many different five-digit numbers can be formed?

2 Algebra II

Exercise 2.1 Factorising

1 Factorise the following expressions.

   (i) $ab + bc + ac + c^2$ **(ii)** $p^2 + pq + pr + qr$ **(iii)** $a^2 + ab + ac + bc$

2 Factorise the following expressions.

   (i) $2ab + 3ac - 4b^2 - 6bc$ **(ii)** $2r^2 + 6rs - 3rt - 9st$

   (iii) $3g^2 - gh - 6gk + 2hk$

3 Factorise the following expressions.

   (i) $x^2 + 5x + 6$ **(ii)** $x^2 - 7x + 10$ **(iii)** $x^2 - 3x - 10$

   (iv) $p^2 + 9p + 14$ **(v)** $r^2 - 15r + 36$ **(vi)** $t^2 - 10t - 75$

4 Factorise the following expressions.

   (i) $2a^2 + 5a + 2$ **(ii)** $2x^2 - x - 6$ **(iii)** $3p^2 - 8p - 3$

   (iv) $2a^2 - 13a + 20$ **(v)** $4c^2 + c - 18$ **(vi)** $3x^2 + 10x - 8$

5 Factorise the following expressions.

   (i) $x^2 + 6xy + 8y^2$ **(ii)** $r^2 + 2ar - 15a^2$ **(iii)** $y^2 + 9yz + 20z^2$

   (iv) $a^2 - 5ab - 6b^2$ **(v)** $p^2 + 7pq + 12q^2$ **(vi)** $s^2 - 4st + 4t^2$

6 Factorise the following expressions.

   (i) $2x^2 + 5xy + 3y^2$ **(ii)** $2a^2 - 5ab + 2b^2$ **(iii)** $9p^2 - 6pq + q^2$

   (iv) $2x^2 - 11xy + 5y^2$ **(v)** $3a^2 - 4ab + b^2$ **(vi)** $6p^2 + 5pq - 6q^2$

7 Factorise the following expressions. (You do not need to expand any brackets in order to do this.)

   (i) $x^2 - 4y^2$ **(ii)** $a^2 - (b + 2)^2$ **(iii)** $(p + 3)^2 - 4q^2$

   (iv) $s^2 - 9(t + 2)^2$ **(v)** $(x - 1)^2 - 16y^2$ **(vi)** $(2x - 1)^2 - y^2$

8 Factorise fully the following expressions.

   (i) $x^3 - 9x$ **(ii)** $a^4 - 4a^2$ **(iii)** $4p^3 - 16p$

   (iv) $4(a + b)^2 - (a - b)^2$ **(v)** $(p + 2q)^2 - (p - 2q)^2$ **(vi)** $4(x + y)^2 - 9(x - y)^2$

Exercise 2.2 Rearranging mathematical formulae

In this exercise all the equations refer to formulae used in mathematics.

1 Make x the subject of $x^2 + y^2 = r^2$.

2 Make h the subject of $A = \frac{1}{2}bh$.

3 Make b the subject of $P = 2(l + b)$.

4 Make r the subject of $V = \frac{4}{3}\pi r^3$.

5 Make l the subject of $A = \pi r^2 + \pi rl$.

6 Make   **(i)** h **(ii)** b the subject of $A = \frac{1}{2}(b + c)h$.

7 Make   **(i)** h **(ii)** r the subject of $V = \pi r^2 h$.

8 Make **(i)** y **(ii)** x the subject of $V = \frac{1}{3}x^2y$.

9 Make **(i)** a **(ii)** u the subject of $v^2 - u^2 = 2as$.

10 Make **(i)** h **(ii)** a the subject of $A = \frac{(a+b)}{2}h$.

Exercise 2.3 Rearranging more general formulae and equations

1 Make p the subject of $2p + 3q = 4pq$.

2 Make t the subject of $2(a + t) = 3(2t - b)$.

3 Make r the subject of $pr = 2(p - r)$.

4 Make c the subject of $6b - 2c = 3bc$.

5 Make d the subject of $a(d - 2) = 2b(3 - 2d)$.

6 Make a the subject of $b = \frac{2a - 3}{3 + 2a}$.

7 Make x the subject of $y = \frac{x - 1}{2x + 1}$.

8 Make s the subject of $p = \frac{2s + 3a}{s}$.

9 Make w the subject of $x = \frac{w + 2}{w - 3}$.

10 Make p the subject of $3p + 2a = \frac{2p}{3 - a}$.

Exercise 2.4 Simplifying algebraic fractions

Simplify the following.

1 **(i)** $\dfrac{3ab^3}{6a^2b}$ **(ii)** $\dfrac{12a^2b^3}{9a^3c^2}$ **(iii)** $\dfrac{6x^2y}{4xy^2}$

2 **(i)** $\dfrac{2x + 4}{4x + 2}$ **(ii)** $\dfrac{3x - 9}{x^2 - x - 6}$ **(iii)** $\dfrac{x^2 + 3x - 18}{2x - 6}$

3 **(i)** $\dfrac{4x^2 - 9}{6x^2 - 13x + 6}$ **(ii)** $\dfrac{x^2 + 2x - 8}{x^2 - 6x + 8}$ **(iii)** $\dfrac{6x^2 - 13x + 6}{9x^2 - 4}$

4 **(i)** $\dfrac{4x^2 - 1}{3x} \times \dfrac{2x}{2x^2 + 3x + 1}$ **(ii)** $\dfrac{3x^2 + 5x - 2}{6x + 3} \times \dfrac{2x + 1}{2x^2 + 3x - 2}$

   (iii) $\dfrac{x + 3}{x^2 - 9} \times \dfrac{x^2 + 2x - 15}{x^2 + 3x - 10}$ **(iv)** $\dfrac{x - 2}{x^2 - x - 6} \times \dfrac{x^2 + 4x + 4}{x^2 + x - 6}$

5 **(i)** $\dfrac{3x}{10x - 4} \div \dfrac{4x^2}{5x - 2}$ **(ii)** $\dfrac{2a - 3}{3a - 2} \div \dfrac{4a - 6}{6a - 4}$

   (iii) $\dfrac{x + 3}{x^2 - 9} \div \dfrac{2x^2 + 5x + 3}{3x^2 + x - 2}$ **(iv)** $\dfrac{x^2 - 4}{x^2 - 2x} \div \dfrac{x^2 - 4x + 4}{x + 2}$

6 **(i)** $\dfrac{4p}{3} + \dfrac{3p}{4}$ **(ii)** $\dfrac{4}{3p} + \dfrac{3}{4p}$ **(iii)** $\dfrac{4p}{3} + \dfrac{3}{4p}$

7 **(i)** $\dfrac{3}{4a + 3} + \dfrac{4}{3a + 2}$ **(ii)** $\dfrac{a}{2a + 3} + \dfrac{a}{2a - 3}$ **(iii)** $\dfrac{a}{a + b} + \dfrac{b}{a - b}$

8 (i) $\dfrac{3x}{2} - \dfrac{2x}{3}$ (ii) $\dfrac{4}{3x} - \dfrac{3}{4x}$ (iii) $\dfrac{3x}{2} - \dfrac{2}{3x}$

9 (i) $\dfrac{3}{p^2 + 2p} - \dfrac{2}{p^2 - 2p}$ (ii) $\dfrac{4x}{x^2 - 4} - \dfrac{2}{x + 2}$

(iii) $\dfrac{2x}{(x+1)(x+2)} - \dfrac{3x}{(x+2)(x+3)}$

10 (i) $\dfrac{a+1}{a} + \dfrac{a^2 + 1}{a^2} + \dfrac{a^3 + 1}{a^3}$ (ii) $\dfrac{3x + y}{3} - \dfrac{2x + y}{2} - \dfrac{2x - y}{6}$

Exercise 2.5 Solving linear equations involving fractions

Solve the following equations.

1 (i) $x + \dfrac{x}{3} = \dfrac{3}{4}$ (ii) $\dfrac{x}{4} + \dfrac{2x}{5} = \dfrac{13}{10}$ (iii) $\dfrac{3x}{2} + \dfrac{2x}{3} = 5$

2 (i) $x - \dfrac{x}{3} = \dfrac{3}{4}$ (ii) $\dfrac{2x}{3} - \dfrac{x}{5} = 7$ (iii) $\dfrac{3x}{2} - \dfrac{2x}{3} = 5$

3 (i) $\dfrac{x+1}{4} + \dfrac{x-1}{2} = 4$ (ii) $\dfrac{2x}{3} - \dfrac{x-1}{5} = 3$ (iii) $\dfrac{x+1}{2} + \dfrac{3x-1}{4} = 9$

4 (i) $\dfrac{x+1}{5} - \dfrac{x}{6} = 1$ (ii) $\dfrac{x}{6} - \dfrac{x+1}{5} = \dfrac{1}{10}$ (iii) $\dfrac{2x-1}{3} + \dfrac{x+2}{4} = 2$

5 (i) $\dfrac{3}{x} - \dfrac{2}{x} = 10$ (ii) $\dfrac{3}{x} + \dfrac{2}{x} = 10$ (iii) $\dfrac{3}{x} - \dfrac{4}{3x} = 10$

6 (i) $\dfrac{3}{2x} - \dfrac{2}{3x} = 5$ (ii) $\dfrac{3+x}{2x} - \dfrac{2+x}{3x} = 1$ (iii) $\dfrac{3-x}{2x} + \dfrac{2-x}{3x} + 1 = 0$

7 (i) $\dfrac{3}{x} - \dfrac{4}{2x+1} = 1$ (ii) $1 + \dfrac{1}{x+1} = \dfrac{2x}{x+1}$ (iii) $\dfrac{2}{2x+1} - \dfrac{3}{3x+1} + \dfrac{1}{2} = 0$

8 (i) $\dfrac{3(p+2)}{5} + 2 = p$ (ii) $q - \dfrac{3(q+1)}{4} = 1$ (iii) $\dfrac{2(r+1)}{3} + \dfrac{(r+2)}{5} = 1$

Exercise 2.6 Completing the square

1 Work out the values of a and b such that $x^2 + 6x + 12 \equiv (x + a)^2 + b$.

2 Work out the values of c and d such that $x^2 - cx + 9 \equiv (x - 2)^2 + d$.

3 Work out the values of p and q such that $4 - 2x - x^2 \equiv p - (x + q)^2$.

4 Work out the values of r and s such that $6 + 4x - x^2 \equiv r - (x + s)^2$.

5 Work out the values of a, b and c such that $3x^2 + ax + 7 \equiv b(x + 2)^2 - c$.

6 Work out the values of p, q and r such that $2x^2 - 12x + 23 \equiv p(x - q)^2 + r$.

7 Work out the values of a, b and c such that $1 - ax - bx^2 \equiv 3 - c(x + 1)^2$.

8 Work out the values of p, q and r such that $p + q(x + r)^2 \equiv 5x^2 - 20x + 16$.

9 (i) Work out the values of a and b such that $x^2 + 6x + 20 \equiv (x + a)^2 + b$.

(ii) Hence make x the subject of $y = x^2 + 6x + 20$.

10 (i) Work out the values of p, q and r such that $4x^2 - 16x + 11 \equiv p(x + q)^2 + r$.

(ii) Hence make x the subject of $y = 4x^2 - 16x + 11$.

3 Algebra III

Exercise 3.1 Function notation

1 $f(x) = x + 2$ and $g(x) = x^2 + 2$

Work out the value of

(i) $f(-2)$ (ii) $f(0)$ (iii) $f(2)$

(iv) $g(-2)$ (v) $g(0)$ (vi) $g(2)$.

2 $f(x) = 2x^2$ and $g(x) = \dfrac{2}{x}$

Work out the value of

(i) $f(-3)$ (ii) $f(3)$

(iii) $g(-3)$ (iv) $g(3)$.

3 $f(x) = 2x - 3$ and $g(x) = 3x - 2$

Work out the value of x when

(i) $f(x) = 0$ (ii) $g(x) = 0$ (iii) $f(x) = g(x)$.

4 $f(x) = 3x + 2$ and $g(x) = 2x - 3$

Solve

(i) $f(x) - g(x) = 0$ (ii) $f(x) + g(x) = 0$ (iii) $f(x) = 2g(x)$.

5 $f(x) = x^2 - 1$ and $g(x) = 2x - 2$

Solve

(i) $f(x) - g(x) = 0$ (ii) $f(x) + g(x) = 0$ (iii) $f(x) = [g(x)]^2$.

6 $f(x) = 2x + 3$

Write down expressions, giving your answers in the simplest form, for

(i) $f(2x + 1)$ (ii) $f(x - 1)^2$ (iii) $[f(x - 1)]^2$.

7 $f(x) = 2x^2 + 3x + 1$

Write down expressions, giving your answers in the simplest form, for

(i) $f(2x)$ (ii) $f(-2x)$

(iii) $f(2x)^2$ (iv) $f(2x^2)$.

8 $f(x) = \dfrac{x^2 - 4}{3}$

(i) Work out the value of $f(4)$.

(ii) Work out the value of x when (a) $f(x) = 0$ (b) $f(x) = 4$.

9 $f(x) = \dfrac{x - 4}{5}$

(i) Work out the value of $f(0)$.

(ii) Work out the value of x when (a) $f(x) = 0$ (b) $f(x) = f(2x)$.

10 $f(x) = \dfrac{2x - 3}{2x + 3}$

   (i) Work out the value of x when **(a)** $f(x) = 0$ **(b)** $f(x) = 2$.

   (ii) Explain why it is not possible for $f(x)$ to equal 1.

11 $f(x) = (3x + 2)^2$

   Write down expressions, giving answers in the simplest form, for

   (i) $f(2x)$ **(ii)** $f(x - 2)$ **(iii)** $(f(x) - 4)^2$.

Exercise 3.2 Domain and range of a function

1 Write down the range of $f(x)$ in each of the following.

   (i) $f(x) = 2x$ $x \leqslant 2$

   (ii) $f(x) = x + 2$ $x \leqslant 2$

   (iii) $f(x) = \dfrac{x}{2}$ $x \leqslant 2$

   (iv) $f(x) = x - 2$ $x \leqslant 2$

2 Write down the range of $f(x)$ in each of the following.

   (i) $f(x) = 5 - x$ $x \geqslant 4$

   (ii) $f(x) = 5 - 2x$ $x \geqslant 4$

   (iii) $f(x) = 5 - 3x$ $x \geqslant 4$

   (iv) $f(x) = 5 - 4x$ $x \geqslant 4$

3 Write down the range of $f(x)$ in each of the following.

   (i) $f(x) = \dfrac{x}{2} - 1$ $2 < x < 4$

   (ii) $f(x) = \dfrac{x - 1}{2} - 1$ $2 < x < 4$

   (iii) $f(x) = \dfrac{x}{2} + 3$ $2 < x < 4$

   (iv) $f(x) = \dfrac{x - 1}{2} + 3$ $2 < x < 4$

   (v) $f(x) = \dfrac{4 - 3x}{2}$ $0 \leqslant x \leqslant 4$

   (vi) $f(x) = \dfrac{5 - 2x}{3}$ $-2 \leqslant x \leqslant 4$

4 Write down the range of $f(x)$ in each of the following.

   (i) $f(x) = x^2$ $0 \leqslant x \leqslant 4$

   (ii) $f(x) = x^2$ $-2 \leqslant x \leqslant 4$

   (iii) $f(x) = x^3 - 2$ $0 \leqslant x \leqslant 4$

   (iv) $f(x) = x^3 + 2$ $-4 \leqslant x \leqslant 4$

5 In each of the following, a sketch of a function f(x) is shown.

Write down the domain and the range for f(x).

(i)

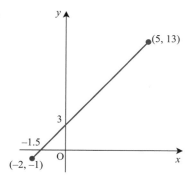

(ii)

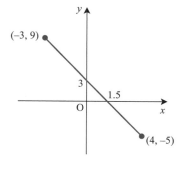

(iii)

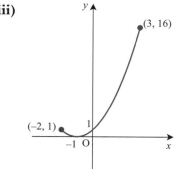

(iv)

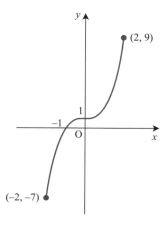

6 A sketch is drawn for each of the curves in parts **(i)** to **(iv)**. Use this sketch to work out the range of the function in the given interval.

(i)   f(x) = x^2 + x

$-3 < x < 2$

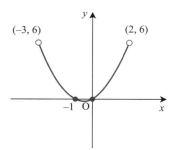

(ii) f(x) = x^2 − x

$-3 < x < 2$

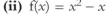

(iii) f(x) = x^2 + x + 3

$-3 < x < 2$

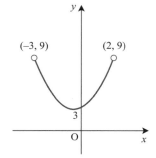

(iv) f(x) = x^2 + x − 4

$-3 < x < 2$

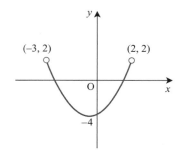

7 In each of parts **(i)** to **(iv)** a sketch of a function, f(x), is shown.
   Write down the range of the function in the given interval.

(i)   −2 < x < 3

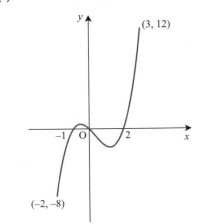

(ii) −2 < x < 4

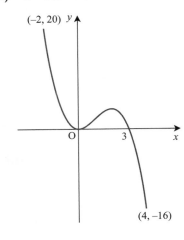

(iii) −2 < x < 1

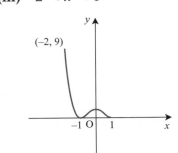

(iv) −3 < x < 1

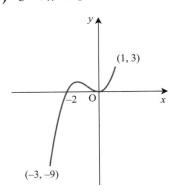

8 A graph of a function is shown in each of parts **(i)** to **(iv)**. Use this graph
   to work out the range of the function in the given interval.

(i)

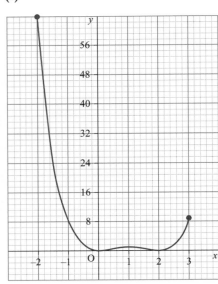

(ii)

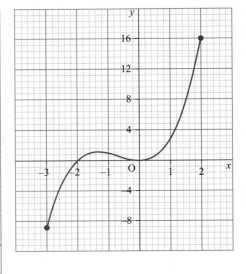

(iii)

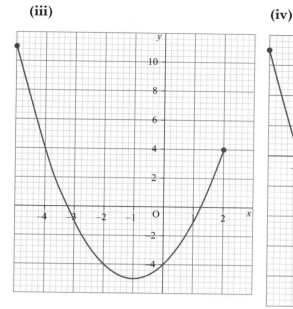

(iv)

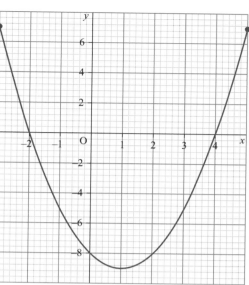

Exercise 3.3 Composite functions

1 Express $(2 - x)^3$ in the form fg(x), stating the expressions corresponding to f(x) and g(x).

2 Given that f$(x) = x - 2$ and g$(x) = x^2 - 2$,

  (i) write **(a)** fg(x) **(b)** gf(x)

  (ii) work out the value of **(a)** fg(2) **(b)** gf(2)

  (iii) work out the value of x when fg(x) = gf(x).

3 Given that f$(x) = 2x$ and g$(x) = 2 + x$,

  (i) write **(a)** fg(x) **(b)** gf(x)

  (ii) calculate as a function of x, **(a)** fg(2) **(b)** gf(2)

  (iii) work out the value of x when f(x) = g(x).

4 The following functions are composite functions.
For each, define g(x) and h(x) such that f(x) = gh(x).

  (i) f$(x) = \sqrt{1 + x}$ **(ii)** f$(x) = (1 - x)^2$ **(iii)** f$(x) = \dfrac{1}{1 + x}$

5 The following functions are composite functions.
For each, define g(x), h(x) and k(x) such that f(x) = ghk(x).

  (i) f$(x) = \sqrt{1 + 3x}$ **(ii)** f$(x) = (1 - 2x)^3$ **(iii)** f$(x) = \dfrac{1}{1 - 4x}$

6 The following functions are composite functions.
For each, define g(x) and h(x) such that f(x) = gh(x).

  (i) f$(x) = \sin 4x$ **(ii)** f$(x) = \cos(x - 45°)$ **(iii)** f$(x) = \dfrac{1}{2}\tan x$

7 The following functions are composite functions.
For each, define g(x), h(x) and k(x) such that f(x) = ghk(x).

  (i) f$(x) = 3\tan 4x$ **(ii)** f$(x) = \dfrac{1}{2}\sin(x + 30°)$ **(iii)** f$(x) = \dfrac{2}{\cos 3x}$

8 Functions f and g are defined so that $f(x) = x^2$ and $g(x) = ax - 2$, where a is a constant.

   (i) Define fg(x) and gf(x).

   (ii) If $a = 2$, work out the values of x for which fg(x) = gf(x) and state the range of values for which fg(x) < gf(x).

   (iii) If $a = 1$, show that there is only one value of x for which fg(x) = gf(x) and work out this value.

   (iv) Show that $f(x)$ and $g(x)$ cannot be equal if $a = 0$.

9 Simon and Lisa have decided to redecorate their lounge. They have bought all the materials and written the following list of what needs to be done.

   (a) Paint the ceiling

   (b) Undercoat the wooden surfaces

   (c) Strip off the old wallpaper

   (d) Wallpaper all the walls

   (e) Top coat the wooden surfaces with gloss paint

There is a preferred order for performing these tasks.

Treating each task as a function, write down the composite function for decorating the room.

(Remember that the function performed first will appear at the end of the list.)

Exercise 3.4 Graphs of linear functions

1 For each of the following pairs of points, A and B, calculate the gradient of the line AB.

   (i) A(2, 4)   B(4, 8)   **(ii)** A(3, 5)   B(5, 5)

   (iii) A(2, 4)   B(7, 6)   **(iv)** A(3, 6)   B(6, 0)

   (v) A(2, 9)   B(5, 3)   **(vi)** A(6, 7)   B(2, 2)

   (vii) A(–2, 3)   B(2, 6)   **(viii)** A(3, –4)   B(–7, 6)

   (ix) A(–2, –1)   B(–1, –2)   **(x)** A(–2, 0)   B(0, –4)

In the following questions mark the coordinates of all points of intersection with the axes.

2 On the same axes, sketch these lines.

   (i) $x = 1$ **(ii)** $x = -2$ **(iii)** $x = 0$

3 On the same axes, sketch these lines.

   (i) $y = 1$ **(ii)** $y = -2$ **(iii)** $y = 0$

4 On the same axes, sketch these lines.

   (i) $y = x$ **(ii)** $y = x + 2$ **(iii)** $y = x - 4$

5 On the same axes, sketch these lines.

   (i) $y = 2x$ **(ii)** $y = 2x + 2$ **(iii)** $y = 2x - 5$

6 On the same axes, sketch these lines.

   (i) $y = x$ **(ii)** $y = 2x$ **(iii)** $y = -x$ **(iv)** $y = -2x$

7 On the same axes, sketch these lines.

   (i) $y = \dfrac{1}{2}x - 2$ **(ii)** $y = 2x - \dfrac{1}{2}$ **(iii)** $y = 3(x - 1)$

8 On the same axes, sketch these lines.

    (i) $x + 2y = 3$ **(ii)** $x - 2y = 3$ **(iii)** $3x - y = 2$

9 On the same axes, sketch these lines.

    (i) $2x + y - 5 = 0$ **(ii)** $x - 3y + 2 = 0$ **(iii)** $3x + 4y - 7 = 0$

10 On the same axes, sketch these lines.

    (i) $\dfrac{x}{3} + \dfrac{y}{2} + 2 = 0$ **(ii)** $\dfrac{2x}{3} - \dfrac{3y}{2} - 6 = 0$ **(iii)** $\dfrac{3x}{2} - \dfrac{2y}{3} + 1 = 0$

11 An electrician charges a fixed call-out fee of £50, and £25 per hour for any work done.

    (i) Write down a formula for the cost £C when a job takes t hours.

    (ii) Work out the cost of a job taking 3 hours.

    (iii) Work out how long the job takes if the total cost is £250.

Exercise 3.5 Finding the equation of a line

1 Work out the equations of the lines **(i)** to **(iv)** in this diagram.

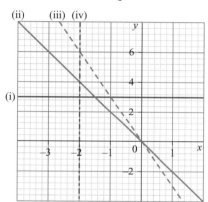

2 Work out the equations of the lines **(i)** to **(vi)** in this diagram.

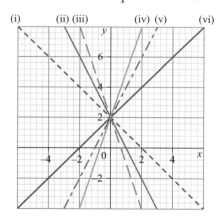

3 Work out the equations of the lines **(i)** to **(v)** in this diagram.

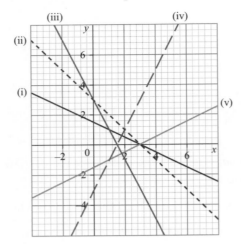

4 Work out the equations of these lines.

   (i) Gradient 1 and passing through $(2, 5)$

   (ii) Gradient 2 and passing through $(-1, 3)$

   (iii) Gradient 3 and passing through $(3, -1)$

   (iv) Gradient 4 and passing through $(-2, -5)$

5 Work out the equations of these lines.

   (i) Gradient -1 and passing through $(-1, 2)$

   (ii) Gradient -2 and passing through $(-2, -1)$

   (iii) Gradient -3 and passing through $(-1, -4)$

   (iv) Gradient -4 and passing through $(5, 0)$

6 Work out the equation of the line AB in each of these cases.

   (i) A(2, 3)   B(3, 2)   **(ii)** A(2, 4)   B(6, 4)

   (iii) A(3, 5)   B(5, 1)   **(iv)** A(1, 6)   B(4, 5)

7 Work out the equation of the line AB in each of these cases.

   (i) A(−1, 2)   B(2, −1)   **(ii)** A(−2, 4)   B(2, −4)

   (iii) A(−1, −2)   B(−2, −1)   **(iv)** A(−2, −4)   B(−4, −2)

8 Triangle ABC has an angle of $90°$ at B. Point A is on the y-axis, AB is part of the line $x - 2y + 6 = 0$ and C is the point $(6, 1)$.

   (i) Sketch the triangle.

   (ii) Work out the equations of AC and BC.

   (iii) Work out the lengths of AB and BC and hence work out the area of the triangle.

9 The total cost of a meal and a bottle of wine is £32.75 and the total cost of two meals and a bottle of wine is £53.75.

   (i) How much does a meal cost?

   (ii) How much does a bottle of wine cost?

10 A taxi journey costs £x plus 90 pence per mile.
A journey of 3 miles costs £5.70.

    (i)   What is the cost of a journey of 7 miles?

    (ii) How far is a journey which costs £12?

Exercise 3.6 Graphs of quadratic functions

1   There are four quadratic curves shown
on the right, and four equations below.
Choose the two equations that match
the curves labelled **(a)** and **(b)**.

    (i) $y = x^2 + 3$

    (ii) $y = 4x - x^2$

    (iii) $y = 4 - x^2$

    (iv) $y = x^2 - 2x + 3$

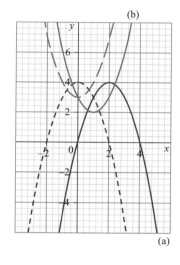

2   Choose an equation from the list below
to fit the quadratic curves **(a)** and **(b)**.

    (i) $y = x^2 - 3x + 6$

    (ii) $y = x^2 + 6$

    (iii) $y = x^2 + 3x + 6$

    (iv) $y = x^2 - 6x + 6$

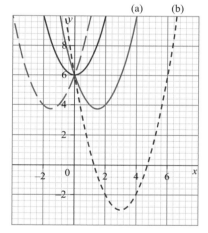

3   Choose an equation from the list below
to fit the quadratic curves **(a)** and **(b)**.

    (i) $y = 4 - x^2$

    (ii) $y = -x^2 + 4x - 4$

    (iii) $y = -x^2 + 2x - 1$

    (iv) $y = 1 - x^2$

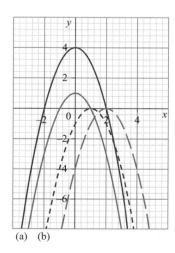

4 **(i)** For the graph of $y = x^2 - 2x - 4$, work out

    (a) the vertex

    (b) the equation of the line of symmetry

    (c) the coordinates of the point where the curve intersects the y-axis.

  (ii) Sketch the graph.

5 **(i)** For the graph of $y = x^2 - 4x + 2$, work out

    (a) the vertex

    (b) the equation of the line of symmetry

    (c) the coordinates of the point where the curve intersects the y-axis.

  (ii) Sketch the graph.

6 **(i)** For the graph of $y = x^2 + 2x - 4$, work out

    (a) the vertex

    (b) the equation of the line of symmetry

    (c) the coordinates of the point where the curve intersects the y-axis.

  (ii) Sketch the graph.

7 **(i)** Write $y = 2x^2 + 4x - 7$ in the form $y = a(x + b)^2 + c$ and for its graph work out

    (a) the vertex

    (b) the equation of the line of symmetry

    (c) the coordinates of the point where the curve intersects the y-axis.

  (ii) Sketch the graph.

8 **(i)** Write $y = 2x^2 - 2x - 5$ in the form $y = a(x - b)^2 + c$ and for its graph work out

    (a) the vertex

    (b) the equation of the line of symmetry

    (c) the coordinates of the point where the curve intersects the y-axis.

  (ii) Sketch the graph.

9 **(i)** Write $y = 4 + 6x - x^2$ in the form $y = a + (x + b)^2$ and for its graph work out

    (a) the vertex

    (b) the equation of the line of symmetry

    (c) the coordinates of the point where the curve intersects the y-axis.

  (ii) Sketch the graph.

10 Work out the equation of each of the following graphs.

(i)
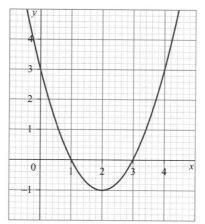

(ii)
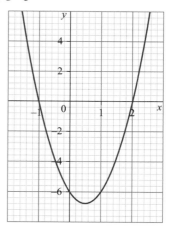

(iii)
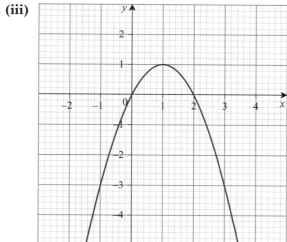

Exercise 3.7 Inverse functions

1 (i) Use a flow chart to work out the inverse of the function $f(x) = \dfrac{2x - 3}{4}$.

(ii) Sketch the graphs of $y = f(x)$ and $y = f^{-1}(x)$ on the same axes.

(iii) What do you notice?

2 (i) Work out the inverse of the function $f(x) = 3x + 2$.

(ii) Sketch $y = f(x)$, $y = x$, and $y = f^{-1}(x)$ on the same axes, using the reflection property to help you sketch the inverse.

(iii) Work out $ff^{-1}(3)$ and $f^{-1}f(3)$.

(iv) What do you notice?

3 (i) Work out the inverse of the function $f(x) = \dfrac{2 - 3x}{4}$.

(ii) Sketch $y = f(x)$, $y = x$, and $y = f^{-1}(x)$ on the same axes, using the reflection property to help you sketch the inverse.

4 (i) Work out the inverse of the function $f(x) = x^2 - 9$ for $x \geqslant 0$.

(ii) Sketch $y = f(x)$, $y = x$, and $y = f^{-1}(x)$ on the same axes, using the reflection property to help you sketch the inverse.

5 (i) Work out the inverse of the function $f(x) = (x + 2)^2$ for $x \geqslant -2$.

(ii) Sketch $y = f(x)$, $y = x$, and $y = f^{-1}(x)$ on the same axes, using the reflection property to help you sketch the inverse.

6 (i) Work out the inverse of the function $f(x) = 3\sqrt{x}$ for $x \geqslant 0$.

(ii) Sketch $y = f(x)$, $y = x$, and $y = f^{-1}(x)$ on the same axes, using the reflection property to help you sketch the inverse.

7 (i) Work out the inverse of the function $f(x) = \dfrac{3}{x}$ for $x > 0$.

(ii) Sketch $y = f(x)$, $y = x$, and $y = f^{-1}(x)$ on the same axes, using the reflection property to help you sketch the inverse.

8 By first finding an expression for the inverse function, work out the value of $f^{-1}(-3)$ when

(i) $f(x) = 3x - 2$

(ii) $f(x) = 2x - 3$

(iii) $f(x) = \dfrac{3 + 4x}{2}$.

9 By first finding an expression for the inverse function, work out the value of $f^{-1}(8)$ when

(i) $f(x) = x^2 + 4$ for $x \geqslant 0$

(ii) $f(x) = (x + 4)^2$ for $x \geqslant -4$

(iii) $f(x) = 4x^2 - 3$ for $x \geqslant 0$.

10 By first finding an expression for the inverse function, work out the value of $f^{-1}(3)$ when

(i) $f(x) = 3\sqrt{x}$ for $x \geqslant 0$

(ii) $f(x) = \dfrac{3}{\sqrt{x}}$ for $x > 0$.

Exercise 3.8 Graphs of exponential functions

1 Sketch the graphs of $y = 2^x$ and $y = 4^x$ on the same axes.

2 Sketch the graphs of $y = 2^x$ and $y = \dfrac{1}{2^x}$ on the same axes.

3 Sketch the graphs of $y = 1^x$, $y = 2^x$ and $y = 3^x$ on the same axes.

4 Sketch the graphs of $y = 2^x$, $y = 2^x - 2$ and $y = 2^x + 2$ on the same axes.

5 Sketch the graphs of $y = 3^x$ and $y = 2 \times 3^x$ on the same axes.

6 Use any graphing software at your disposal to draw the graphs of $y = 3^x \div 2$ and $y = 2^x \div 3$ on the same axes.

7 Use any graphing software at your disposal to draw the graphs of $y = 3^x \div 2$ and $y = (3 \div 2)^x$ on the same axes.

8 A parachutist jumps out of an aeroplane and after a few seconds opens the parachute. Her speed, t seconds from when the parachute opens is given by $v\,\mathrm{m\,s^{-1}}$ where $v = 5 + 20 \times 3^{-0.1t}$.

(i) What is her speed when the parachute opens?

(ii) What is her speed after 10 seconds?

(iii) What is her speed after 1 minute?

(iv) Sketch the graph of v against t.

9 The number, N, of insects in a colony is given by $N = 500 \times 2^{0.01t}$ where t is the time in days after the colony was first discovered.

   (i) How many insects were there initially?

   (ii) How many insects are there after 20 days?

   (iii) Sketch the graph of N against t, marking the points found in parts **(i)** and **(ii)** on your sketch.

10 A radioactive material decays according to the law $m = 20 \times (0.5)^t$ where m grams is the mass after t days.

   (i) What is the mass initially?

   (ii) Sketch the graph of m against t for $0 \leqslant t \leqslant 5$.

   (iii) Use trial and improvement to work out the number of days until the mass is less than 0.1 grams.

Exercise 3.9 Graphs of functions with up to three parts to their domains

1 Draw the graph of $y = f(x)$, where
$$\begin{aligned} f(x) &= 3 & -2 \leqslant x < 3 \\ &= x & 3 \leqslant x \leqslant 5 \end{aligned}$$

2 Draw the graph of $y = f(x)$, where
$$\begin{aligned} f(x) &= -x & -2 \leqslant x < 0 \\ &= x & 0 \leqslant x \leqslant 2 \end{aligned}$$

3 Draw the graph of $y = f(x)$, where
$$\begin{aligned} f(x) &= x + 2 & -2 \leqslant x < 0 \\ &= 2 - x & 0 \leqslant x \leqslant 2 \end{aligned}$$

4 Draw the graph of $y = f(x)$, where
$$\begin{aligned} f(x) &= x + 3 & -3 \leqslant x < -2 \\ &= 1 & -2 \leqslant x < 2 \\ &= 3 - x & 2 \leqslant x \leqslant 3 \end{aligned}$$

5 Draw the graph of $y = f(x)$, where
$$\begin{aligned} f(x) &= 4 & -4 \leqslant x < -2 \\ &= x^2 & -2 \leqslant x < 2 \\ &= 4 & 2 \leqslant x \leqslant 4 \end{aligned}$$

6 Draw the graph of $y = f(x)$, where
$$\begin{aligned} f(x) &= 0 & -2 \leqslant x < -1 \\ &= 1 - x^2 & -1 \leqslant x < 0 \\ &= 1 + x^2 & 0 \leqslant x \leqslant 1 \end{aligned}$$

7 Here is the graph of $y = f(x)$.

 (i) Define $f(x)$, stating clearly the domain for each part.

 (ii) State the range of $f(x)$.

 (iii) Solve $f(x) = 2$.

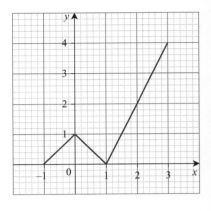

8 Here is the graph of $y = f(x)$.

 (i) Define $f(x)$, stating clearly the domain for each part.

 (ii) State the range of $f(x)$.

 (iii) Work out the area between the graph and the x-axis.

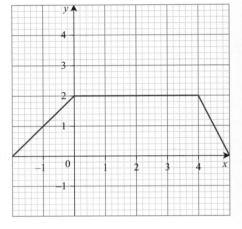

9 Here is the graph of $y = f(x)$.

 (i) Define $f(x)$, stating clearly the domain for each part.

 (ii) State the range of $f(x)$.

 (iii) Work out $f(1)$.

 (iv) Solve $f(x) = 2$. (3 answers)

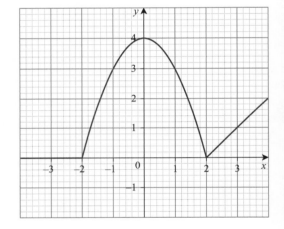

10 In Utopia, the tax on earned income is calculated as follows.
The first £20 000 is tax free, the next £40 000 is taxed at 20% and the remaining income is taxed at 40%.

 (i) Draw a graph of tax against income, with income on the horizontal axis, for incomes up to £100 000.

 (ii) Work out the tax paid by someone earning £36 000 a year.

 (iii) Work out the tax paid by someone earning £75 000 a year.

 (iv) Work out the gross income (i.e. income before tax) received by a person paying £16 000 in tax.

4 Algebra IV

Exercise 4.1 Solving quadratic equations by factorising, completing the square or using the quadratic formula

Where necessary, give the answers in surd form.

1 Solve, by factorising:

   (i) $x^2 - 6x + 8 = 0$ **(ii)** $y^2 - 9y - 10 = 0$

   (iii) $w^2 - 5w = 6$ **(iv)** $2p^2 + 7p - 15 = 0$

   (v) $3n^2 - 20n = 7$ **(vi)** $2m^2 = 5m + 3$

2 Solve, by completing the square:

   (i) $p^2 - 8p + 15 = 0$ **(ii)** $x^2 - 6x - 16 = 0$

   (iii) $m^2 + 2m - 3 = 0$ **(iv)** $2t^2 - 6t - 7 = 0$

   (v) $2y^2 - 11y + 5 = 0$ **(vi)** $3n^2 - 4n = 2$

3 Solve, using the quadratic formula:

   (i) $y^2 + 5y - 9 = 0$ **(ii)** $p^2 - 3p - 5 = 0$

   (iii) $m^2 + 8m + 2 = 0$ **(iv)** $2r^2 + 6r - 9 = 0$

   (v) $5n^2 - 2n = 7$ **(vi)** $3w^2 = 2 - 8w$

4 Solve

   (i) $\dfrac{2}{x} + \dfrac{x-2}{3} = \dfrac{7}{6}$ **(ii)** $\dfrac{m}{3} + \dfrac{12}{m-2} = 5$

   (iii) $\dfrac{a}{4} - \dfrac{6}{a+1} = 3$ **(iv)** $\dfrac{y+3}{2} + \dfrac{4}{2y-5} = 7$

   (v) $\dfrac{6}{n} + \dfrac{4}{n-1} = 7$ **(vi)** $\dfrac{5}{p+2} + \dfrac{1}{2p+1} = 6$

5 Solve

   (i) $\dfrac{x+3}{2x-1} = \dfrac{13-x}{x+4}$ **(ii)** $\dfrac{w+2}{w-1} = \dfrac{2w-1}{2w+3}$

   (iii) $\dfrac{p-3}{1-2p} = \dfrac{p+2}{5-p}$ **(iv)** $\dfrac{2y-5}{y+1} = \dfrac{3y+7}{y-3}$

   (v) $\dfrac{5t-1}{2t+3} = \dfrac{t+1}{t-2}$ **(vi)** $\dfrac{3a+1}{a-3} = \dfrac{6-a}{4-2a}$

PS **6** The sides of a right-angled triangle, in centimetres, are $x + 1$, $2x$ and $2x + 1$.

   (i) Explain why $2x + 1$ must be the length of the hypotenuse.

   (ii) Hence work out the area of the triangle.

PS **7** Given that $v^2 - 2kv = 4k^2$, write k in terms of v.

PS **8** The two roots of the quadratic equation $3x^2 + 5x + p = 0$ are equal.

   Work out the value of p.

Exercise 4.2 Solving simultaneous equations

1 Solve each pair of simultaneous equations by elimination.

   (i) $3x + y = 8$
         $4x - y = 6$

   (ii) $3p + 8q = 7$
         $3p + 11q = 4$

   (iii) $5m + n = 14$
         $3m - 4n = -10$

   (iv) $2a + 3b = 7$
         $a - 6b = 11$

   (v) $2r + 3s = -1$
         $3r - 5s = 27$

   (vi) $4c - 3d = 11$
         $5c = 13 + 7d$

2 Solve each pair of simultaneous equations by substitution.

   (i) $y = x + 1$
         $y = 2x - 3$

   (ii) $y = 7x - 4$
         $y = 3x + 4$

   (iii) $y = 5x + 1$
         $2x + 3y = 20$

   (iv) $4x + 3y = 11$
         $y = 2x - 13$

   (v) $2x + y = 7$
         $3x + 2y = 15$

   (vi) $3x - 4y = 23$
         $x + 7y = -9$

3 Solve each pair of simultaneous equations.

   (i) $y = x + 3$
         $y = x^2 - x - 5$

   (ii) $y = x - 2$
         $y = x^2 - 3x - 7$

   (iii) $y = 2x - 1$
         $y = x^2 + 3x - 3$

   (iv) $y = x + 1$
         $x^2 - y^2 = 7$

   (v) $2x + y = 3$
         $x^2 + y^2 = 5$

   (vi) $2x^2 - y^2 = 41$
         $x + 3y = -4$

4 The straight line $y = x + 4$ intersects the ellipse $9x^2 + 4y^2 = 180$ twice.

   Work out the coordinates of the two points of intersection.

PS 5 The area of a rectangle is $9\,cm^2$.

   The length of one of its diagonals is $\sqrt{30}$ cm.

   Work out its perimeter in the form $\sqrt{a}$ cm.

PS 6 The sum of two numbers is 6.

   The product of the two numbers is 7.

   Work out the difference between the two numbers.

PS 7 $4 + \sqrt{34}$ and $4 - \sqrt{34}$ are the roots of the equation $x^2 + ax + b = 0$. Work out the values of a and b.

PS 8 p and q are the two roots of the quadratic equation $x^2 - 8x + a = 0$.

   If the difference between p and q is 14, then work out the value of a.

Exercise 4.3 Factor theorem

1 Show that

   (i) $(x - 1)$ is a factor of $x^3 - 4x + 3$

   (ii) $(x + 2)$ is a factor of $x^4 - 16$

   (iii) $(x - 3)$ is a factor of $x^3 - x - 24$

   (iv) $(x + 4)$ is a factor of $x^3 + 2x^2 + 32$.

2 Show that

    (i) $(2x - 1)$ is a factor of $2x^3 + 3x^2 - 1$

    (ii) $(2x + 3)$ is a factor of $2x^3 - 5x^2 - 4x + 12$

    (iii) $(3x + 1)$ is a factor of $9x^4 - x^2 + 6x + 2$

    (iv) $(2x + 1)$ is a factor of $8x^4 + 2x^2 - 1$.

3 **(i)** Show that $(x - 1)$ is a factor of $x^3 - 3x + 2$.

    (ii) Hence fully factorise $x^3 - 3x + 2$.

4 $f(x) = x^3 - 4x^2 + x + 6$

    (i) Calculate $f(2)$.

    (ii) Hence fully factorise $f(x)$.

5 $g(x) = x^3 - 5x^2 + 5x + 3$

    (i) Show that $(x - 3)$ is a factor of $g(x)$.

    (ii) Hence solve $g(x) = 0$.

6 $(x + 2)$ is a factor of $x^5 - ax^2 + 8 = 0$.

    Work out the value of a.

PS **7** $(x + 2)$ and $(x - 4)$ are two factors of $x^3 + 3x^2 + px + q$.

    Work out the third factor.

PS **8** $(x + 1)$ is a factor of $x^4 + 3x^3 + px + q$.

    $(x - 2)$ is a factor of $x^3 - px^2 + qx + 9$.

    Work out the values of p and q.

Exercise 4.4 Linear inequalities

1 Solve the following inequalities.

    (i) $3x + 7 > 5$ **(ii)** $5 - 2x < 9$

    (iii) $4x + 3 \leqslant 7x - 2$ **(iv)** $2(3x - 4) \geqslant x + 4$

    (v) $7(x - 2) > 3(x + 5)$ **(vi)** $4(x + 3) \leqslant 2(3x - 7) + 6$

2 Work out the values of x that satisfy both inequalities $2x + 1 > 0$ and $3x - 5 \leqslant 0$.

3 Solve the following inequalities.

    (i) $\dfrac{2x + 3}{5} < 7$ **(ii)** $6 \leqslant \dfrac{3 - x}{4}$

    (iii) $\dfrac{x + 1}{3} \geqslant x - 2$ **(iv)** $2x + 1 > \dfrac{x - 4}{2}$

    (v) $\dfrac{3 - x}{2} < \dfrac{5 - 2x}{3}$ **(vi)** $\dfrac{5 - x}{6} \geqslant \dfrac{x + 1}{2}$

4 Solve the following inequalities.

    (i) $2 \leqslant x + 3 \leqslant 5$ **(ii)** $4 < 3x + 1 \leqslant 10$

    (iii) $2 < 5 - x < 11$ **(iv)** $-1 \leqslant 3 - 2x < 9$

    (v) $3 < \dfrac{x - 2}{5} \leqslant 4$ **(vi)** $-1 \leqslant \dfrac{x}{4} - 1 < 9$

5 Given that $1 \leqslant p \leqslant 3$ and $2 \leqslant q \leqslant 7$, work out the inequalities for

(i) $p + q$ (ii) $p - q$

(iii) $2p + q$ (iv) $p - 3q$.

6 Given that $-4 \leqslant m \leqslant 3$ and $-2 \leqslant n < 5$, work out the inequalities for

(i) m^2 (ii) $m + n$

(iii) $m^2 - n^2$ (iv) n^3.

7 Given that $x < 0$ and $y > 0$, decide whether the following statements are ALWAYS TRUE, SOMETIMES TRUE or NEVER TRUE.

(i) $2x > 1$ (ii) $x + y < 0$

(iii) $xy < 0$ (iv) $y - x > 0$

(v) $x^2 > 0$ (vi) $y < 5$

8 Given that $0 < w < 1$, $x < 0$ and $y < 1$, decide whether the following statements are ALWAYS TRUE, SOMETIMES TRUE or NEVER TRUE.

(i) $3w < 1$ (ii) $wxy < 0$

(iii) $\dfrac{wx}{y} \leqslant -6$ (iv) $0 < wx < 1$

(v) $\dfrac{w}{x} < 0$ (vi) $-3 < w + x + y < 3$

Exercise 4.5 Quadratic inequalities

1 Solve the following inequalities.

(i) $x^2 - 4x + 3 > 0$ (ii) $x^2 + 7x + 6 \leqslant 0$ (iii) $x^2 - 3x - 4 \geqslant 0$

(iv) $x^2 - 5x \leqslant 14$ (v) $x^2 + 7 < 8x$ (vi) $80 - x^2 > 2x$

2 Solve the following inequalities (expressing your answers in terms of surds where necessary).

(i) $4x^2 - 3x - 1 \geqslant 0$ (ii) $2x^2 - x - 1 < 0$ (iii) $2x^2 < x + 3$

(iv) $3x^2 + 2 \geqslant 7x$ (v) $x^2 + 3x > 7$ (vi) $2x^2 \leqslant 3x + 9$

3 For which values of x are the following graphs below the x-axis?

(i) $y = x^2 - 3x + 2$ (ii) $y = x^2 - 1$ (iii) $y = 2x^2 - 3x + 1$

(iv) $y = 9 - x^2$ (v) $y = 3 + 2x - 5x^2$ (vi) $y = 2 + x - 4x^2$

4 The dimensions (in cm) of a triangle and a rectangle are shown in the diagram. If the area of the triangle is greater than the area of the rectangle, work out the possible values of x.

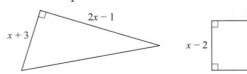

5 (i) Solve $3(y + 2) > y - 12$

(ii) Solve $y^2 \geqslant 4$

(iii) Hence work out the values of y for which both inequalities are satisfied.

6 (i) Solve $(x + 4)(x - 2) < 0$

(ii) Solve $(x + 1)(x - 5) \leqslant 0$

(iii) Hence work out the values of x for which both inequalities are satisfied.

PS 7 **(i)** Solve $x^2 - 4x + 3 \leqslant 0$

(ii) Solve $y^2 - 6y + 8 < 0$

(iii) Hence, given that $w = x + y$, work out an inequality for w.

PS 8 Given that $p^2 < 9$ and $q^2 - 3q \leqslant 10$, work out an inequality for m, where $m = 2p - q$.

PS 9 For which values of x is the graph of $y = 2x^2 - 5$ below the graph of $y = x^2 - x - 3$?

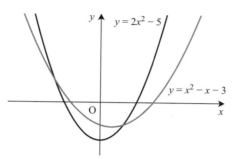

Exercise 4.6 Indices

1 Write as single powers of x.

(i) $\dfrac{x^2 \times x^7}{x^5}$

(ii) $\dfrac{x^3}{x^7 \times x^4}$

(iii) $x^{\frac{1}{2}} \times x^{\frac{1}{3}} \times x^{\frac{1}{6}}$

(iv) $\sqrt{x^4 \times x^8 \div x^5}$

(v) $\sqrt[3]{x^4 \times x^{11}}$

(vi) $\sqrt{\left(x^3\right)^6}$

(vii) $\left(\sqrt{x}^{-5}\right)^4$

(viii) $\sqrt[4]{\dfrac{x^3 \times x^7}{x^8 \times x^5}}$

2 Expand and simplify.

(i) $x^2(x^3 + x^{-4})$

(ii) $x^{\frac{1}{2}}\left(2x^{\frac{1}{2}} + x^{-\frac{1}{2}}\right)$

(iii) $x^{-1}(x - 3x^{-2})$

(iv) $\sqrt[3]{x}\left(x^{\frac{2}{3}} - 4x^{\frac{5}{3}}\right)$

(v) $\sqrt[4]{x}\left(3x^{1.75} + x^{-\frac{1}{4}}\right)$

3 Solve, giving solutions as exact values.

(i) $x^{-1} = 7$

(ii) $x^{\frac{1}{2}} = 9$

(iii) $x^{-2} = \dfrac{1}{4}$

(iv) $x^{-\frac{1}{3}} = -\dfrac{2}{3}$

(v) $x^{-3} = 8$

(vi) $x^{\frac{2}{3}} = 16$

(vii) $x^{-\frac{1}{2}} = 4$

(viii) $x^{-\frac{3}{2}} = 27$

4 **(i)** Solve $3^y - 1 = 0$. **(ii)** Hence solve $(3^{x+2} - 1)(3^x - 81) = 0$.

5 **(i)** Use a suitable substitution to show that the equation $4^x = 2^{x+1} + 8$ can be written as $y^2 - 2y - 8 = 0$.

(ii) Hence solve $4^x = 2^{x+1} + 8$.

6 Solve $x + 3 + \dfrac{2}{x} = 0$.

7 Solve $x + 6 = 5\sqrt{x}$.

PS 8 Solve $(x^2 - 3)^{x-3} = 1$.

Exercise 4.7 Algebraic proof

1 (i) Prove that the product of any two odd numbers is always odd.

   (ii) Prove that the product of any two even numbers is always even.

2 (i) Complete the square for the expression $x^2 - 2x + 3$.

   (ii) Hence show that $x^2 - 2x + 3$ is positive for all values of x.

3 Given that $f(x) = x^2$ prove that $f(y + 4) - f(y)$ is a multiple of 8 for all y.

4 Prove that the product of two consecutive integers added to the higher integer is always a square number.

5 (i) Prove that all even square numbers are multiples of 4.

   (ii) Prove that all odd square numbers are one more than a multiple of 4.

6 Prove that a square number can never be one less than a multiple of 3.

7 (i) Show that $x^2 - 2xy + y^2 \geqslant 0$ for all values of x and y.

   (ii) Hence show that $(x + y)^2 \geqslant 4xy$ for all values of x and y.

   (iii) Hence show that $\dfrac{x + y}{2} \geqslant \sqrt{xy}$ for all positive x and y.

8 (i) Write $\dfrac{x}{y} + \dfrac{y}{x}$ as a single fraction.

   (ii) Show that $x^2 - 2xy + y^2 \geqslant 0$ for all values of x and y.

   (iii) Hence show that $\dfrac{x}{y} + \dfrac{y}{x} \geqslant 2$ for all positive x and y.

Exercise 4.8 Linear sequences

1 Work out an expression for the nth term for each of the following linear sequences.

   (i) $5, 8, 11, 14, \ldots$

   (ii) $6, 10, 14, 18, \ldots$

   (iii) $10, 20, 30, 40, \ldots$

   (iv) $7, 2, -3, -8, \ldots$

   (v) $0, -3, -6, -9, \ldots$

   (vi) $-5, -9, -13, -17, \ldots$

2 Work out the 100th term of each of these linear sequences.

   (i) $4, 6, 8, 10, \ldots$

   (ii) $6, 11, 16, 21, \ldots$

   (iii) $10, 19, 28, 37, \ldots$

   (iv) $6, -1, -8, -15, \ldots$

   (v) $0, -8, -16, -24, \ldots$

   (vi) $-7, -9, -11, -13, \ldots$

3 For each of these linear sequences, work out the value of the first term of the sequence that is greater than 250.

    (i)   2, 8, 14, 20, …

    (ii)   7, 10, 13, 16, …

    (iii) 11, 20, 29, 38, …

    (iv) −7, −2, 3, 8, …

    (v) 0, 3, 6, 9, …

    (vi) −5, −1, 3, 7, …

4 Work out the value of the first negative term in each of these linear sequences.

    (i)   74, 66, 58, 50, …

    (ii) 100, 97, 94, 91, …

    (iii) 4000, 3994, 3988, 3982, …

    (iv) 2000, 1991, 1982, 1973, …

    (v) 500, 488, 476, 464, …

    (vi) 987, 980, 973, 966, …

PS **5** p is the first number of a linear sequence.
q is the second number of the same sequence.

    (i) Write the third number in terms of p and q.

    (ii) Write the nth number in terms of p, q and n.

    (iii) Given that the 10th number is 74, write an equation connecting p and q.

    (iv) Given also that the 12th number is 88, work out the values of p and q.

PS **6** The nth term of a sequence is $7n + 2$.
Explain why 654 is not a term in the sequence.

PS **7** The nth term of a sequence is n^2.
Prove that the difference between consecutive terms is always odd.

PS **8** a, b and c are the first three terms respectively of a linear sequence.

Work out an expression for b in terms of a and c.

Exercise 4.9 Quadratic sequences and the limiting value of a sequence

1 Calculate the next term of each quadratic sequence.

    (i)   1, 2, 4, 7, 11, …

    (ii) 4, 8, 14, 22, 32, …

    (iii) 3, 6, 11, 18, 27, …

    (iv) 15, 13, 10, 6, 1, …

2 Work out the nth term for each of the following quadratic sequences.

    (i) $2, 5, 10, 17, 26, \ldots$

    (ii) $5, 9, 15, 23, 33, \ldots$

    (iii) $1, 3, 7, 13, 21, \ldots$

    (iv) $3, 5, 9, 15, 23, \ldots$

    (v) $5, 9, 17, 29, 45, \ldots$

    (vi) $30, 29, 22, 9, -10, \ldots$

PS 3 $5, 8, p, 26, 41$ are the 1st, 2nd, 3rd, 4th and 5th terms of a quadratic sequence, respectively.

    (i) Calculate the value of p.

    (ii) Hence, or otherwise, work out the nth term of the sequence.

4 The nth term of a sequence is $\dfrac{3 - 2n}{3n + 4}$.

    (i) Calculate the first three terms of the sequence.

    (ii) Write down the limiting value of the sequence as $n \to \infty$.

PS 5 The nth term of a sequence is $\dfrac{an + 5}{2n - 1}$.

    The limiting value of the sequence as $n \to \infty$ is -3.

    (i) Write down the value of a.

    (ii) Calculate the first term of the sequence.

6 $3, 11$ and 25 are the first three terms of a quadratic sequence.

    Work out the nth term of the sequence.

PS 7 The nth term of a sequence is $\dfrac{4n^2 - 5n + 6}{7 + 4n - 11n^2}$.
Work out its limiting value.

> Divide the numerator and denominator by n^2.

PS 8 $2, p, 12, q, 30$ is a quadratic sequence.

    Work out the values of p and q.

Exercise 4.10 Simultaneous equations in three unknowns

1 Solve the simultaneous equations:

$$x + y + z = 12$$
$$2x + y + z = 23$$
$$x + 2y + z = 25$$

2 Solve the simultaneous equations:

$$3x + y - z = -4$$
$$x + 2y + z = 6$$
$$2x - 3y + 4z = 4$$

PS 3 $(x - 1)$ and $(x + 1)$ are factors of $x^3 + px^2 + qx + r$.

    (i) Work out the value of q.

    (ii) Given also that $p = r + 6$, work out the values of p and r.

4 Solve the simultaneous equations:

$$2x + 5y = z + 19$$
$$3x + 4z = 2y - 11$$
$$x + 3y - 14 = 2z$$

5 Solve the simultaneous equations $y = x - 5$, $z = 5 - 3y$ and $x = 3 - 4z$.

6 The nth term of a sequence is $\dfrac{an + 1}{2n + b}$.

The first term of the sequence is -3, and its limiting value as $n \to \infty$ is 4.

Work out the value of the 3rd term.

PS **7** Explain why these simultaneous equations have no solution.

$$2x + y - 3z = 1$$
$$4x + 2y - 6z = 5$$
$$2x - y + 3z = 2$$

PS **8** The nth term of a sequence is given by $an^2 + bn + c$.
The 2nd, 3rd and 5th terms of the sequence are -4, -4 and 2 respectively.

(i) Write down three equations in a, b and c.

(ii) Solve the equations in part **(i)** to work out the nth term of the sequence.

5 Coordinate geometry

Exercise 5.1 Parallel and perpendicular lines: distances, midpoints and gradients

> In all questions involving axes we assume the same scale on both axes, unless otherwise stated.

1 For each of the following pairs of points A and B, work out

  (a) the gradient of the line AB

  (b) the gradient of the line perpendicular to AB

  (c) the length of AB

  (d) the coordinates of the midpoint of AB

(i)	A(2, 1)	B(4, 7)	**(ii)**	A(2, 3)	B(5, 9)
(iii)	A(5, 2)	B(−3, 2)	**(iv)**	A(0, 7)	B(5, 8)
(v)	A(−2, 6)	B(4, 3)	**(vi)**	A(−5, −3)	B(2, 4)
(vii)	A(−9, 2)	B(0, −2)	**(viii)**	A(4, −6)	B(6, −4)

2 A(3, 4), B(6, 1) and C(10, 5) are the vertices of a triangle.

  (i) Draw the triangle.

  (ii) Show that the triangle is right-angled by finding the lengths of the sides.

  (iii) Show that the triangle is right-angled by finding the gradients of the sides.

  (iv) Work out the area of the triangle.

3 A triangle has vertices A(4, 0), B(6, 4) and C(−1, 5).

  (i) Draw the triangle.

  (ii) Show that the triangle is isosceles.

  (iii) Work out the area of the triangle.

4 A triangle has vertices (−3, 4), (7, 4) and (6, 1). Work out

  (i) the lengths of the sides of the triangle and hence show that the triangle is right-angled

  (ii) the area of the triangle.

5 The three points A(1, 4), B(x, 1) and C(9, 0) are collinear (i.e. they lie on the same straight line).

  (i) Work out the value of x.

  (ii) Work out the ratio of the lengths AB : BC.

6 A quadrilateral has vertices A(0, 0), B(4, 4), C(6, 2) and D(2, −2). Work out the type of quadrilateral by calculating the gradients and lengths of the sides.

7 A quadrilateral has vertices A(−4, 3), B(−1, 4), C(5, 2) and D(5, 0).

  (i) Draw the quadrilateral.

  (ii) Using appropriate calculations, work out the type of quadrilateral.

  (iii) Work out the possible coordinates of the point E when ABCE is a parallelogram.

8   A triangle has vertices A(−1, 2), B(4, −1) and C(1, −2.5).

   (i)   Draw the triangle.

   (ii) Work out the coordinates of the point D so that ABCD is a parallelogram.

9   A triangle has vertices A(−1, −1), B(1, 2) and C(4, 0).

   (i)   Draw the triangle.

   (ii) Give two words that describe the triangle and, in each case, show why this is true.

10 A quadrilateral has vertices A(2, 3), B(4, 5), C(6, 3) and D(4, −2).

   (i)   Draw the quadrilateral.

   (ii) Show by calculation that ABCD is a kite.

   (iii) Work out the area of the kite.

   E is the point (4, 2).

   (iv) Work out the area of ABCE and hence state the area of AECD.

11 The vertices of a triangle are A(7, 3), B(−4, 1) and C(−3, −2).

   (i)   Show that the triangle is isosceles.

   (ii) Work out the midpoint of BC.

   (iii) Work out the area of the triangle.

12 The points A(1, 3), B(5, 7), C(4, 8) and D(x, y) form a rectangle.

   (i)   Show A, B and C on a diagram.

   (ii) Work out the coordinates of D and hence calculate the area of the rectangle.

13 The perpendicular bisector of a line AB is the line that is perpendicular to AB and passes through its midpoint.

   (i)   Write, in terms of p and q, the coordinates of the midpoint of the line joining A(p, q) and B(q, p).

   (ii) Show that the origin is on the perpendicular bisector of the line AB.

14 A(3, −1), B(6, 0), C(7, 3) and D(4, 2) are the vertices of a quadrilateral.

   (i)   Sketch the quadrilateral and specify the type of quadrilateral.

   (ii) Prove that the diagonals bisect each other at right angles.

   (iii) Work out the area of the quadrilateral.

15 The vertices of a triangle are A(a, 0), B(0, b) and C(c, d) and angle ABC = 90°
    Write the relationship between a, b, c and d.

| You may find it helpful
to use graph paper for
Question 16. |

16 A quadrilateral has vertices A(−3, −1), B(−1, 3), C(5, 5) and D(6, 2).
    Draw the quadrilateral and hence calculate its area.

Exercise 5.2 Equations of straight lines

1   By calculating the gradients of the following pairs of lines, state whether they are parallel, perpendicular or neither.

   (i) $x = 3$ $y = 3$

   (ii) $y = 3x + 2$ $y = 3x − 2$

   (iii) $y = 4 − 2x$ $y = 4 + 2x$

(iv) $x + 2y = 4$ $\qquad$ $x - 2y = 4$

(v) $x - 2y = 3$ $\qquad$ $y - 2x = 4$

(vi) $3x - 2y + 5 = 0$ $\qquad$ $3x - 2y - 7 = 0$

(vii) $x = 2y$ $\qquad$ $2x + y = 3$

(viii) $2x + 5y = 7$ $\qquad$ $5x + 2y = 7$

2 Work out the equations of these lines.

   (i) Parallel to $y = 4x$ and passing through $(3, -1)$

   (ii) Parallel to $y = 5x + 3$ and passing through $(1, -2)$

   (iii) Parallel to $y = 2 - 4x$ and passing through $(5, -3)$

   (iv) Parallel to $2x - 3y = 5$ and passing through $(2, 6)$

   (v) Parallel to $x - 2y + 4 = 0$ and passing through $(-3, -2)$

   (vi) Parallel to $2x + 3y - 6 = 0$ and passing through $(5, -1)$

3 Work out the equations of these lines:

   (i) Perpendicular to $y = 3x$ and passing through $(0, 2)$

   (ii) Perpendicular to $y = 2x - 3$ and passing through $(3, -1)$

   (iii) Perpendicular to $y + x = 2$ and passing through $(-2, 4)$

   (iv) Perpendicular to $2x + 3y = 5$ and passing through $(0, 0)$

   (v) Perpendicular to $3x - 2y = 1$ and passing through $(-3, 2)$

   (vi) Perpendicular to $4x - 3y = 0$ and passing through $(4, -1)$

4 Triangle ABC has an angle of 90° at C. Point A is on the x-axis, B is on the y-axis, AB is part of the line $3x + 2y - 12 = 0$ and C is the point $(5, 5)$.

   (i) Sketch the triangle.

   (ii) Work out the coordinates of A and B.

   (iii) Calculate the area of the triangle.

5 The line with equation $3x - 4y + 12 = 0$ cuts the x-axis at A and the y-axis at B.

   (i) Work out the coordinates of A and B.

   (ii) Sketch the line.

   (iii) Work out the area of triangle AOB where O is the origin.

   (iv) Work out the equation of the line perpendicular to AB and passing through O.

   (v) Work out the length of AB and calculate the shortest distance from O to AB.

6 A quadrilateral has vertices at the points A$(-3, -2)$, B$(-3, 0)$, C$(3, 2)$ and D$(3, 0)$.

   (i) Sketch the quadrilateral.

   (ii) Work out the gradient of each side and hence identify the type of quadrilateral.

   (iii) Work out the area of the quadrilateral.

   (iv) Work out the gradient of AC and hence calculate the acute angle between the two diagonals of the quadrilateral, giving your answer to 1 d.p.

7 A right-angled isosceles triangle has two of its vertices at the origin O(0, 0) and the point A(4, 3). The right angle is at (0, 0).

(i) Sketch two possible positions of the triangle on the same diagram.

(ii) B is the vertex to the left of A. Work out the lengths of the sides OA, OB and AB.

(iii) Work out the equations of the three sides of the triangle OAB.

(iv) Work out the coordinates of the other possible vertex C

(v) Explain why the triangle ABC is also isosceles and calculate its area.

8 When the mortgage rate was 4% a small building society lent £240 million, but when the rate dropped to 2.4% it lent £400 million. Assume that the graph of amount lent against interest rate is linear for interest rates between 2% and 6%.

(i) Sketch the graph of amount lent (in £million) against interest rates (%) in this interval, with interest rates on the horizontal axis.

(ii) Work out the equation of the line.

(iii) Work out the amount lent if the interest rate is

     (a) 2%   (b) 5%.

9 A student is carrying out an experiment to measure the elasticity of an elastic band. The instructions are to hang different masses on one end, to measure the stretched length, and to repeat this five times, with different masses. However, because of a shortage of time, the experiment is only carried out twice and these pairs of data are used rather than finding a line of best fit for more points. The results are:

Mass in grams (x)	50	100
Length in mm (y)	180	270

Assume that the graph of mass against length is a straight line.

(i) Sketch the graph of length against mass.

(ii) Find the equation of the line.

(iii) Find the unstretched length of the elastic band.

(iv) Find the load which gives an *extension* of 150 mm.

(v) What do you think will happen when a load of 1 kg is attached to the elastic band?

10 Temperature is commonly expressed in degrees Celsius, but there is an alternative scale called Fahrenheit. The freezing point of water can be written as 0 °C or 32 °F and the boiling point as 100 °C or 212 °F. Both of these are linear scales.

(i) Sketch the graph of degrees Celsius on the horizontal axis against degrees Fahrenheit on the vertical axis, using the two pieces of information given.

(ii) Use this information to find a formula that will convert degrees Celcius (c) to degrees Fahrenheit (f)

(iii) What temperature would have the same numerical value on both scales?

Exercise 5.3 The intersection of two lines

You will need graph paper for this exercise.

1 Solve these pairs of simultaneous equations by plotting their graphs. In each case you are given a suitable range of values for x.

(i) $y = x + 1$ $\qquad$ $x + y = 3$ $\qquad$ $-1 \leqslant x \leqslant 4$

(ii) $x + 2y = 4$ $\qquad$ $x - 2y = -2$ $\qquad$ $-2 \leqslant x \leqslant 4$

2 Solve these pairs of simultaneous equations by plotting their graphs. In each case you are given a suitable range of values for x.

(i) $y = x - 3$ $\qquad$ $x + 3y = -1$ $\qquad$ $-1 \leqslant x \leqslant 5$

(ii) $x + 3y = 0$ $\qquad$ $x - 3y + 6 = 0$ $\qquad$ $-6 \leqslant x \leqslant 0$

3 (i) Plot the lines $y = 3$, $x - 2y = 0$ and $x + 2y = 4$ on the same axes for $-2 \leqslant x \leqslant 6$.

(ii) State the coordinates of the three points of intersection, and for each point give the pair of simultaneous equations that are satisfied there.

(iii) Work out the area of the triangle enclosed by the three lines.

(iv) Name the type of triangle.

4 (i) Plot the lines $y = x - 8$ and $2x + y = 7$ on the same axes for $0 \leqslant x \leqslant 9$.

(ii) Calculate the area between these two lines and the x-axis.

(iii) Calculate the area between these two lines and the y-axis.

5 A triangle has vertices A$(-1, 2)$, B$(3, 4)$ and C$(4, 2)$.

(i) Calculate the lengths of the sides of the triangle.

(ii) Calculate the gradients of the sides of the triangle.

(iii) Describe the triangle.

(iv) Calculate the area of the triangle.

6 (i) The coordinates of three vertices of a kite are A$(7, 5)$, B$(4, 2)$ and C$(7, -8)$. Sketch the kite and state the coordinates of the fourth vertex D.

(ii) Which sides of the kite are perpendicular? Show your working out.

(iii) Calculate the area of the kite if 1 unit represents $12\,\text{cm}$.

7 Amanda and Belinda each have a part-time job during two weeks of their summer holidays in order to raise spending money for their holiday away.

Amanda is paid for 14 days work and Belinda, who doesn't work at the weekend, is paid for 10 days. Belinda's job is more skilful and she is paid £2 more per day than Amanda. Together they earn £224.

Work out how much they each earn per day.

8 Michael's parents decided to save all their 10p and 20p coins for their son. After two weeks they decided to see how much had been saved and were delighted with the sum of £7.80 from a total of 48 coins.

How many coins were there of each denomination?

9 The ages of a man and his grandson add up to 80 years. Ten years later the man will be four times as old as his grandson.

How old are they now?

10 Try to solve each of the following using simultaneous equations. Give a reason for what is happening in each case.

   (i) Four pork chops and two lamb chops cost £12 and six pork chops and three lamb chops cost £18.

     Work out the cost of two pork chops and one lamb chop.

   (ii) $2x + y + 3z = 19$ and $x + y + 4z = 17$

     (a) Using simultaneous equation techniques, write x in terms of z and y in terms of z.

     (b) What happens when you substitute these values in an attempt to solve the simultaneous equations?

     (c) Why?

Exercise 5.4 Dividing of a line in a given ratio

1 In each of the following, AB is a straight line and C is a point on AB. Work out the coordinates of C.

   (i) A is $(1, 3)$ B is $(10, 6)$ AC : CB is 2 : 1

   (ii) A is $(-4, 3)$ B is $(2, 0)$ AC : CB is 1 : 2

   (iii) A is $(-2, 10)$ B is $(5, -4)$ AC : CB is 5 : 2

   (iv) A is $(-3, -7)$ B is $(6, 11)$ AC : CB is 2 : 7

2 In each of the following, PQR is a straight line. The coordinates of two points on the line and the ratio PQ : QR are given. In each case, work out the coordinates of the remaining point.

   (i) P is $(1, 3)$ Q is $(3, 4)$ PQ : QR is 2 : 5

   (ii) P is $(20, -4)$ Q is $(15, -3)$ PQ : QR is 5 : 3

   (iii) P is $(-4, -5)$ R is $(6, 0)$ PQ : QR is 4 : 1

   (iv) Q is $(0, -1)$ R is $(4, -5)$ PQ : QR is 3 : 2

3 ABC is a straight line where AB is 50% longer than BC. A is the point $(-3, 7)$ and B is the point $(3, 4)$.

   (i) Draw the line ABC.

   (ii) Work out the ratio AB : BC in its simplest form.

   (iii) Work out the coordinates of C.

4 PQR is a straight line with PR = 3PQ. P is the point $(-3, 7)$ and R is the point $(6, 1)$.

   (i) Draw the line PQR.

   (ii) Work out the coordinates of Q.

5 Work out the ratio in each of the following cases.

   (i) The circumference of a circle to its diameter.

   (ii) The perimeter of a square to the length of a side.

   (iii) The areas of circles with radii 5 cm and 6 cm respectively.

   (iv) The areas of squares with sides of length 5 cm and 6 cm respectively.

6 A man left £150 000 in his will to be divided among his three children in the ratio of their ages at the time of making his will. At this time, Anna was 22, Brian was 26 and Charlotte was 27. How much does each receive?

7 A mother has three children aged 4, 6 and 8. The three children cannot agree on the correct share they should each have of a circular cake. She rules that it should be divided in the same ratio as their ages. How many degrees of cake should each child have?

8 The total cost of building a house may be divided between materials, wages and administrative costs. In 2018 a builder found that, for a particular type of house, these costs were in the ratio 3 : 6 : 1.

   (i) Work out each of these costs for a house that cost £250 000 to build.

   By 2019 the cost of materials had risen by 5%, wages by 4% and administrative costs by 6%.

   (ii) Calculate the new cost of building a similar house and the overall percentage increase in costs.

Exercise 5.5 Equation of a circle

1 Write down the equations of these circles:

   (i) centre $(0, 1)$, radius 3

   (ii) centre $(3, 0)$, radius 5

   (iii) centre $(-2, 5)$, radius 2

   (iv) centre $(4, -3)$, radius 3

   (v) centre $(-6, -2)$, radius 4.

2 For each of the circles given below

   (a) state the coordinates of the centre

   (b) state the radius

   (c) sketch the circle, paying particular attention to its position in relation to the origin and the coordinate axes.

   (i) $x^2 + y^2 = 4$

   (ii) $(x - 2)^2 + y^2 = 9$

   (iii) $x^2 + (y + 3)^2 = 9$

   (iv) $(x - 5)^2 + (y - 5)^2 = 25$

   (v) $(x + 3)^2 + (y - 4)^2 = 25$

3 Write down the equations of these circles:

   (i) centre $(2, 3)$, passing through $(0, 3)$

   (ii) centre $(-1, 2)$, passing through $(2, -1)$

   (iii) centre $(1, -1)$, passing through $(1, 2)$.

4 Show that the equation $x^2 + y^2 + 4x - 6y - 12 = 0$ represents a circle. Hence give the coordinates of the centre, the radius of the circle and sketch the circle.

5 Why does the equation $x^2 + y^2 + 4x - 6y + 19 = 0$ not represent a circle?

6 A and B are the points $(-2, 4)$ and $(6, 10)$ respectively. Work out the equation of the circle that has AB as diameter.

7 A circle of radius 13 cm passes through the points $(2, 0)$ and $(12, 0)$.

    (i) Sketch two possible positions of the circle.

    (ii) The centre of the top circle is A. State the x coordinate of A and hence calculate its y coordinate.

    (iii) State the coordinates of the centre of the bottom circle.

    (iv) Write down the equations of the two circles.

    (v) Work out the points of intersections of the circles with the y-axis, giving your answers to 2 decimal places.

8 Show that the equation $x^2 + y^2 - 6x + 4y + 4 = 4$ represents a circle. Work out the coordinates of the centre and the radius of the circle and write down the equation of a concentric circle with radius 5.

9 A circle with centre $(-1, 1)$ passes through the point $(2, 5)$.

    (i) Work out the equation of the circle.

    (ii) Work out the equation of a circle with the same centre and double the radius.

10 Work out the midpoint, C, of AB where A and B are $(1, 8)$ and $(3, 14)$ respectively. Hence work out the equation of the circle with AB as diameter.

11 A circle passes through the points $(1, 0)$ and $(5, 0)$ and has the y–axis as a tangent. Write down two possible equations for the circle and illustrate these on a sketch.

Exercise 5.6 Circle geometry, including tangents and chords

If a diagram is not given, a sketch may help.

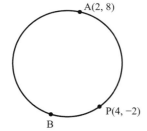

1 AB is a diameter of a circle and P is a point on the circumference. A and P are the points $(2, 8)$ and $(4, -2)$ respectively. Work out the gradient of BP.

2 A$(6, 3)$ and B$(10, 1)$ are two points on a circle with centre $(11, 8)$. Work out

    (i) the coordinates of the midpoint of the chord AB

    (ii) the distance of the chord AB from the centre of the circle

    (iii) the radius of the circle

    (iv) the equation of the circle.

3 The diagram shows the circle $(x - 2)^2 + (y + 3)^2 = 100$.

    (i) Write down the radius of the circle and the coordinates of the centre C.

    (ii) P$(8, y_1)$ and Q$(8, y_2)$ are points on the circumference of the circle. Work out the values of y_1 and y_2.

    (iii) Work out the area of the triangle CPQ.

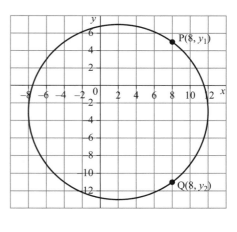

4   The diagram shows the circle
    $(x - 2)^2 + (y + 1)^2 = r^2$ with the
    tangent at the point $(1, 1)$.

    (i) Work out the radius of the circle.

    (ii) Write the equation of the
        tangent at the point $(1, 1)$.

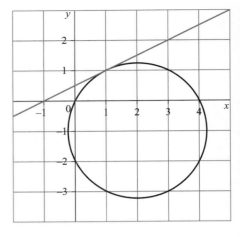

5   A circle with its centre on the y-axis and radius 5, intersects the x-axis at
    $(-3, 0)$ and the positive y-axis at $(0, y)$.

    (i) Work out the value of y, where y is positive.

    (ii) Write the equations of the tangents to the circle at the points $(-3, 0)$
        and $(0, y)$ and work out their point of intersection.

6   A is the point $(-3, 7)$ on the circle with centre, C $(0, 3)$.

    (i) Sketch the circle and work out its radius.

    (ii) B is at the opposite end of the diameter to A, and D is the point $(x, 7)$.
        Work out the coordinates of B and D.

    (iii) Describe the triangle, ABD.

7   **(i)** Sketch the circle $(x - 1)^2 + (y + 2)^2 = 25$.

    (ii) Write the equations of the tangents to the circle at the points $(-2, 2)$
        and $(1, -7)$.

    (iii) Work out the point of intersection of these tangents.

8   A circle has equation $x^2 + y^2 + 10y = 0$.

    (i) Work out the radius of the circle and the coordinates of its centre, C,
        and hence sketch the circle.

    (ii) Write the equation of the tangent to the circle at the point B$(3, -9)$
        and work out the coordinates of the point A, where this tangent
        intersects the x-axis.

    (iii) Sketch the quadrilateral OABC, where O is the origin, and work out
        its area.

9   A circle of radius 3 has its centre at the point D$(0, 3)$. A is the point $(4, 0)$
    and the x-axis is a tangent to the circle. The other tangent to the circle
    from A touches the circle at B.

    (i) Write down the equation of the circle.

    (ii) Sketch the circle and the tangent, AB.

    (iii) Work out the area OABD, where O is the origin.

Geometry I

Exercise 6.1 Circle theorems

1   C is the centre of the circle. Work out angle x.

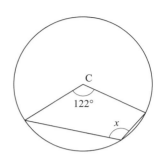

2   PQ is a tangent. Work out angle x.

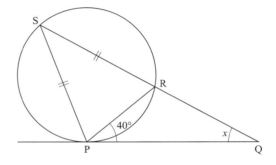

3   C is the centre of the circle and PQ = QS. Work out angle x.

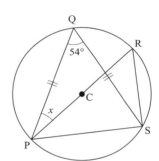

4   C is the centre of the circle. Show that PR bisects ∠QPS.

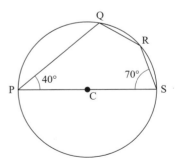

5   Work out the angles of the triangle PQR.

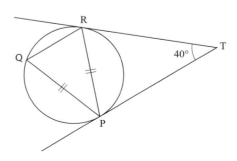

6 The diagram shows a circle, centre O, inscribed in a triangle ABC. Work out ∠RQP.

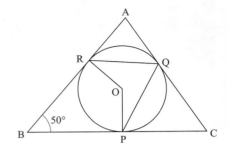

7 Work out the values of x and y given that C is the centre of the circle and the line AB is a tangent.

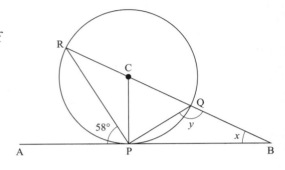

8 (i) PQT is a tangent to the circle. Write down the value of ∠PQR in terms of x.

(ii) Work out the value of x.

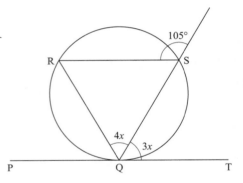

9 C is the centre of the circle and TP is a tangent. Work out angle x.

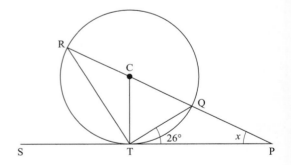

10 C_1 and C_2 are the centres of the two circles.

(i) Work out angle y in terms of x.

(ii) Show that AC_1BC_2 is a cyclic quadrilateral.

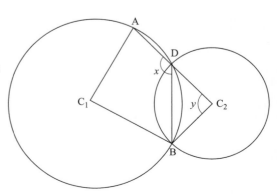

Exercise 6.2 Geometric proof

1 C is the centre of the circle.
   (i)   Work out the other angles in triangles ABC and BCD in terms of x and y.
   (ii) Prove that $\angle ABD = 90°$.

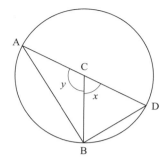

2 C is the centre of the circle.
   Use the diagram above to prove the result 'Angle at the centre is double the angle at the circumference'.

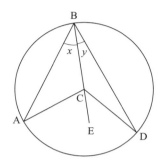

3 C is the centre of the circle.
   Use the result from question 2 to prove that 'Angles in the same segment are equal'.

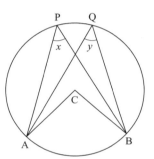

4 C is the centre of the circle and M is the midpoint of the chord AB.
   Prove that $x = 90°$, i.e. the line joining the centre of the circle to the midpoint of a chord is perpendicular to the chord.

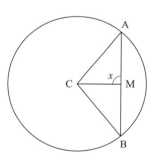

5 Prove that the opposite angles of a parallelogram are equal.

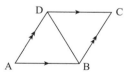

6 C is the centre of the circle.
   Prove that $x + y = 180°$ (i.e. opposite angles of a cyclic quadrilateral add up to $180°$).

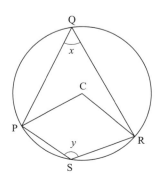

7 AB and AD are tangents to a circle centre C. Prove that AB = AD.

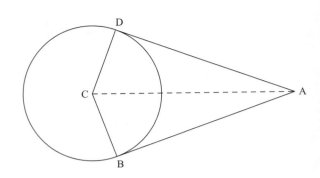

8 PTQ is a tangent to the circle. Prove the alternate segment theorem, i.e. show ∠ BTQ = ∠ BAT. (Hint: add the diameter TCR.)

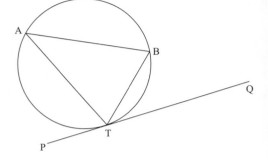

Exercise 6.3 Trigonometry in two dimensions

1 Work out the length marked x in each of these triangles. Give your answers correct to 1 decimal place.

(i)

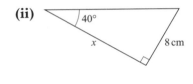

(ii)

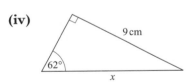

(iii)

(iv)

2 Work out the size of the angle marked θ in each of these triangles. Give your answers correct to 1 decimal place.

(i)

(ii)

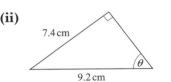

(iii)

(iv)

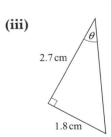
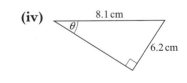

3 In an isosceles triangle the line of symmetry bisects the base of the triangle. Use this fact to work out the angle θ and the lengths x and y in these diagrams. Give your answers correct to 1 decimal place.

(i)

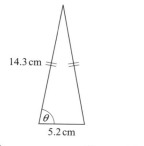

14.3 cm

5.2 cm

θ

(ii)

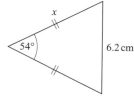

x

54°

6.2 cm

(iii)

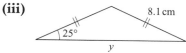

8.1 cm

25°

y

(iv)

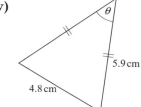

θ

5.9 cm

4.8 cm

4 Calculate, giving your answers correct to 1 decimal place:

(i) Angle ADB

(ii) Angle DCB

(iii) The length AC.

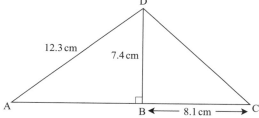

D

12.3 cm

7.4 cm

A

B ← 8.1 cm → C

5 From the top of a vertical cliff 45 m high, a walker can see a llama at an angle of depression of 28°.

(i) Show this information on a sketch.

(ii) Work out how far the llama is from the base of the cliff. (Assume the llama is represented by a point.)

In the next question give answers to the nearest metre.

6 Amberchurch (A) is 5.5 km due South of Brampton (B), and Chapeltown (C) is on a bearing of 050° from Amberchurch. Chapeltown is due East of Brampton.

(i) Show this information on a sketch.

(ii) Work out the distance of Chapeltown from Amberchurch.

(iii) A walker starts from Amberchurch. He wants to visit Brampton and Chapeltown, in either order, walking the shortest possible distance, and then return to Amberchurch by bus. How far, in metres, will he walk?

7 From two points A and B on level ground, the angles of elevation of the top C of a church spire are θ° and 45° respectively, where $\theta < 45$. D is a point on the ground vertically below the top of the spire. AB = 30 m and BD = 50 m.

(i) Show this information on a sketch.

(ii) Work out the height of the spire.

(iii) Work out the value of θ.

8 From two points A and B on level ground, the angles of elevation of the top, T, of a vertical radio mast, ST, which is 60 m high are 23° and 40°, respectively.

(i) Show this information on a sketch.

(ii) Work out the distance BS.

(iii) Work out the distance AB.

Exercise 6.4 Angles of 45°, 30° and 60°

Use of a calculator is not allowed in Exercise 6.4.

1 Work out the exact value of x in each of the following. Give your answers in their simplest form.

(i)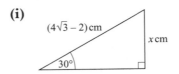

(ii)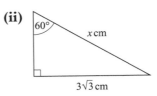

(iii)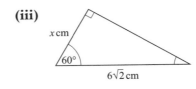

(iv)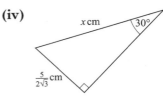

2 Work out the length AB and hence calculate the area of triangle ABC.

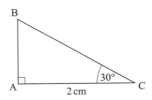

3 ABC is an equilateral triangle of side 6 cm. Work out its area.

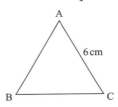

4 Look at the diagram.
   Work out

   (i) the length BD

   (ii) the length DC

   (iii) the area of the triangle ABC.

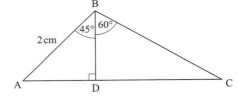

5 A ship travelling with a constant speed of 30 km h^{-1} travels 30 km from A to B on a bearing of 030° and then changes direction to due East for a further 30 km until it reaches C. It then travels directly back to A.

   (i) Show this information on a sketch.

   (ii) Work out the distance from C to A.

   (iii) Work out the total time for the journey in hours and minutes.

6 At midnight, a ship is at a point M travelling at 20 km h^{-1} and sailing due North when it passes two lightships, A and B, which are in a line due East from the ship. Lightship A is closer to the ship than lightship B. At 1 a.m. the ship is at a point N and the bearings of A and B from the ship are 135° and 120°, respectively.

   (i) Show this information on a sketch.

   (ii) Work out the distance from M to A.

   (iii) How far apart are the two lightships?

7 Three survey points P, Q and R are on a North–South line on level ground. P is the most northerly, and from P the foot of a statue, S, 200 metres away is on a bearing of 120°. From Q, S is due East and from R it is on a bearing of 045°.

    (i) Show this information on a sketch.

    (ii) Work out the distances QS and RS.

8 The diagram shows a pyramid on a square base of side 80 cm with equilateral triangles for its four sloping sides.

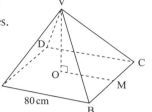

    (i) Sketch the side VBC and calculate its area.

    (ii) Work out the total surface area of the pyramid.

    (iii) Work out the height of the pyramid.

Exercise 6.5 Trigonometric functions for angles of any size, and trigonometric graphs

Give answers to 1 decimal place where necessary.

1 Solve the following equations for $0° \leqslant \theta \leqslant 360°$.

    (i) $\sin \theta = 0.5$ **(ii)** $\cos \theta = \dfrac{\sqrt{3}}{2}$ **(iii)** $\tan \theta = 2$

    (iv) $\cos \theta = -0.5$ **(v)** $\tan \theta = -\sqrt{2}$ **(vi)** $\sin \theta = -\dfrac{\sqrt{3}}{2}$

2 Solve the following equations for $-180° \leqslant \theta \leqslant 180°$.

    (i) $5 \sin \theta = 2$ **(ii)** $9 \cos \theta = 4$ **(iii)** $2 \tan \theta = 7$

    (iv) $4 \cos \theta + 3 = 0$ **(v)** $\tan \theta + 7 = 4$ **(vi)** $5 \sin \theta + 2 = 0$

3 Solve the following equations for $0° \leqslant \theta \leqslant 360°$.

    (i) $\sin^2 \theta = 0.6$ **(ii)** $\cos^2 \theta = 0.4$ **(iii)** $\tan^2 \theta = 10$

4 **(i)** Factorise $3x^2 - x - 2$.

    (ii) Hence solve $3x^2 - x - 2 = 0$.

    (iii) Use your results to solve these equations for $-360° \leqslant \theta \leqslant 360°$.

        (a) $3 \cos^2 \theta - \cos \theta - 2 = 0$

        (b) $3 \sin^2 \theta - \sin \theta - 2 = 0$

        (c) $3 \tan^2 \theta - \tan \theta - 2 = 0$

5 Solve the following equations for $-180° \leqslant \theta \leqslant 180°$.

    (i) $2 \sin^2 \theta + \sin \theta = 1$

    (ii) $2 \tan^2 \theta - 3 \tan \theta - 5 = 0$

    (iii) $8 \cos^2 \theta - 2 \cos \theta - 3 = 0$

    (iv) $4 - 9 \sin^2 \theta = 0$

6 Solve $(2 \sin \theta + 1)(\sin \theta - 2)(\sin \theta - 1) = 0$ for $0° \leqslant \theta \leqslant 360°$.

Do not use a calculator in the following question.

7 Solve the following equations for $-360° \leqslant \theta \leqslant 360°$.

    (i) $\cos \theta = 1$ **(ii)** $\sqrt{2} \cos \theta = 1$ **(iii)** $2 \cos \theta = 1$

    (iv) $\sin \theta = 1$ **(v)** $\sqrt{2} \sin \theta = 1$ **(vi)** $2 \sin \theta = 1$

    (vii) $\tan \theta = 1$ **(viii)** $\tan \theta = \dfrac{1}{\sqrt{3}}$ **(ix)** $\tan \theta = \sqrt{3}$

8 **(i)** Given that $f(x) = 4x^3 + 4x^2 - x - 1$, calculate $f\left(\dfrac{1}{2}\right)$.

   (ii) Hence solve $4\cos^3\theta + 4\cos^2\theta - \cos\theta - 1 = 0$ for $-180° \leqslant \theta \leqslant 180°$.

Exercise 6.6 Trigonometric identities

Give answers to 1 decimal place where necessary.

1 For each of the equations **(i)–(vi)**:

    (a) use the identity $\sin^2\theta + \cos^2\theta \equiv 1$ to rewrite the equation in a form involving only one trigonometric function

    (b) factorise where necessary, and hence solve the resulting equation for $0° \leqslant \theta \leqslant 180°$.

  (i) $2\cos^2\theta + 3\sin^2\theta = 3$ **(ii)** $3\cos^2\theta + 2\sin^2\theta = 3$

  (iii) $\sin^2\theta - \sin\theta = \cos^2\theta$ **(iv)** $\cos^2\theta - \cos\theta = \sin^2\theta$

  (v) $1 - \sin\theta = \cos^2\theta$ **(vi)** $1 - \cos\theta = \sin^2\theta$

2 For each of the equations **(i)–(iv)**:

    (a) use the identity $\sin^2\theta + \cos^2\theta \equiv 1$ to rewrite the equation in a form involving only one trigonometric function

    (b) use the quadratic formula to solve the resulting equation for $0° \leqslant \theta \leqslant 180°$.

  (i) $\sin^2\theta + \cos\theta = 0$ **(ii)** $\cos^2\theta + \sin\theta = 0$

  (iii) $2\sin^2\theta + \cos\theta = 0$ **(iv)** $4\sin^2\theta - 5\cos\theta + 2 = 0$

3 **(i)** Use the identity $\tan\theta \equiv \dfrac{\sin\theta}{\cos\theta}$ to rewrite the equation $\cos\theta = 4\sin\theta$ in terms of $\tan\theta$.

  (ii) Hence solve $\cos\theta = 4\sin\theta$ for $0° \leqslant \theta \leqslant 180°$.

4 Use the identity $\tan\theta \equiv \dfrac{\sin\theta}{\cos\theta}$ to solve the following equations for $0° \leqslant \theta \leqslant 360°$.

  (i) $\tan\theta - \dfrac{2\cos\theta}{\sin\theta} = 0$ **(ii)** $\sin\theta + 2\cos\theta = 0$

  (iii) $2\sin\theta + 3\cos\theta = 0$ **(iv)** $5\cos\theta - 2\sin\theta = 0$

5 Write the following in terms of $\cos\theta$.

  (i) $\tan^2\theta\,\cos^3\theta$

PS   **(ii)** $\sin\theta\,(2\sin\theta - \tan\theta)$

PS 6 Simplify $\dfrac{1}{\cos^2 x} - 1$.

PS 7 Prove the following identities.

  (i) $(\cos x + \sin x)^2 + (\cos x - \sin x)^2 \equiv 2$

  (ii) $\left(\dfrac{1}{\tan x} + \dfrac{1}{\sin x}\right)^2 \equiv \dfrac{1 + \cos x}{1 - \cos x}$

8 **(i)** Simplify the expression $\dfrac{1}{1 + \cos x} + \dfrac{1}{1 - \cos x}$.

  (ii) Solve $\dfrac{1}{1 + \cos x} + \dfrac{1}{1 - \cos x} = 4$ for $0° \leqslant x \leqslant 360°$.

9 Solve the equation $\dfrac{1}{\cos x} + \tan^2 x = 5$ for $0° \leqslant x \leqslant 360°$.

7 Geometry II

Exercise 7.1 The area of a triangle

Where necessary, leave answers approximated to 1 decimal place.

1 Work out the area of each triangle.

(i)
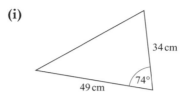

(ii)
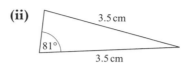

2 Work out the value of x for each triangle.

(i)
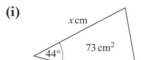

(ii)
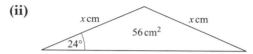

(iii)
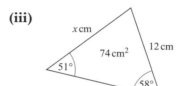

3 Work out the area of an equilateral triangle with side length 9 cm.

4 Work out the side length of an equilateral triangle with area 23 cm².

5 Work out angle x for each triangle.

(i)
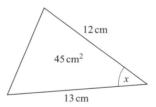

(ii)
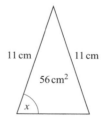

6 Work out the value of x in this triangle.
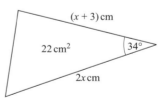

7 Work out the value of w in this triangle.
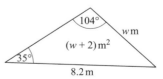

8 The area of triangle PQR is $(2a + 1)$ cm².
Work out the possible values of a.
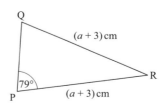

51

PS **9** The area of a regular hexagon is $12\sqrt{3}$ cm². Work out the length of each side of the hexagon.

PS **10** A parallelogram has sides of length 12 m and 7 m. One of its angles is 105°. Work out the area of the parallelogram.

PS **11** The area of a parallelogram is 32 cm². Two of the sides of the parallelogram are 8 cm and 13 cm. Work out the angles of the parallelogram.

Exercise 7.2 The sine rule

Where necessary, leave answers approximated to 1 decimal place.

1 Work out the length x in each of these triangles.

(i)

(ii)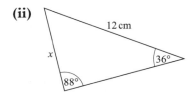

2 Work out the length y in each of these triangles.

(i)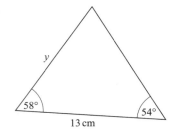

(ii)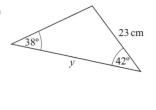

3 Work out the size of the angle θ in each of these triangles.

(i)

(ii)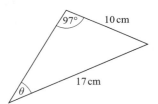

4 Triangle ABC is drawn such that AB = 7 cm, BC = 8 cm, and angle ACB = 37°.

  (i) Work out the possible sizes of angle BAC.

  (ii) If angle BAC is obtuse, work out the size of angle ABC.

5 Triangle PQR is drawn such that QR = 9 cm, angle PRQ = 47°, and angle PQR = 58°.

  (i) Work out the length of side PR.

  (ii) Hence work out the area of triangle PQR.

6 Triangle LMN is drawn such that LM = 12 cm, MN = 13 cm, and angle MLN = 51°.

  (i) Work out angle MNL.

  (ii) Hence work out the area of triangle LMN.

PS 7 The diagram shows a triangle divided into two smaller triangles.

Work out the exact value of sin θ.

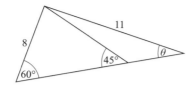

PS 8 Triangle WXY is drawn such that WX = 23 cm, XY = 10 cm, and angle XYW = 70°. Point Z lies on side WY such that angle XZY = 40°.

Work out the area of triangle WXZ.

PS 9 Triangle ABC has area 100 cm², and side BC = 15 cm. Point D lies on the side AC such that angle ADB = 80° and angle CBD = 35°.

Work out the area of triangle ABD.

Exercise 7.3 The cosine rule

Where necessary, leave answers approximated to 1 decimal place.

1 Work out the length x in each triangle.

(i)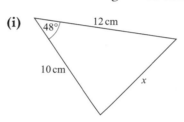

(ii)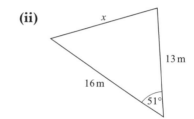

2 Work out the angle θ in each triangle.

(i)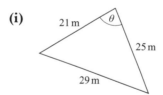

(ii)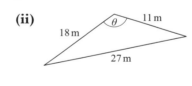

3 A triangle has sides of length 9 cm, 12 cm and 13 cm.

   (i) Work out the size of the largest angle.

   (ii) Work out the size of the smallest angle.

4 Triangle PQR is drawn such that PQ = 7.3 cm, QR = 8.6 cm, and angle PQR = 56°.

   (i) Work out the length PR.

   (ii) Work out the area of triangle PQR.

5 Triangle XYZ is drawn such that XZ = 10 m, XY = 11 m, YZ = x and angle XYZ = 60°.

   (i) Use the cosine rule to show that $x^2 - 11x + 21 = 0$.

   (ii) Hence work out two possible areas of triangle XYZ.

PS 6 A rhombus has sides of length 7 cm. Two of the angles of the rhombus are 110°.

   (i) Work out the length of the longer diagonal.

   (ii) Work out the length of the shorter diagonal.

   (iii) Hence work out the area of the rhombus.

PS 7 Nick cycles 3 km on a bearing of 070°, followed by 7 km on a bearing of 120°.

Work out the direct distance between his final and start positions.

PS 8 The three side-lengths of a triangle are $8x$, $x + 1$ and $8x + 1$.

If the largest angle is 150°, work out the exact value of x.

Exercise 7.4 Using the sine and cosine rules together

Where necessary, leave answers approximated to 1 decimal place.

1 Triangle ABC is drawn such that AB = 12 cm, BC = 14 cm and angle ABC = 60°.

   (i) Work out the length AC.

   (ii) Work out angle ACB.

   (iii) Work out the area of triangle ABC.

2 Triangle DEF is drawn such that DE = 9.5 cm, angle DEF = 54° and angle EDF = 71°.

   (i) Work out the length EF.

   (ii) Work out the length DF.

   (iii) Work out the area of triangle DEF.

PS 3 A triangle has sides of length 7.3 cm, 8.4 cm and 9.3 cm.

Work out the area of the triangle.

PS 4 Linda walks 4 km on a bearing of 065°, followed by 6 km on a bearing of 110°.

   (i) Work out the direct distance between Linda's original and final positions.

   (ii) Work out Linda's new bearing from her original position.

PS 5 A parallelogram has sides of length 5.3 cm and 7.2 cm. Two of the angles are 102°.

   (i) Work out the length of the shorter diagonal.

   (ii) Work out the area of the parallelogram.

PS 6 Two sides of an acute triangle have lengths 6.7 cm and 8.3 cm.
The area of the triangle is 23 cm².
Work out the length of the third side.

PS 7 The diagonals of a parallelogram are 9.3 cm and 7.2 cm.
The acute angle between the diagonals is 61°.

   (i) Work out the area of the parallelogram.

   (ii) Work out the length of the longest side of the parallelogram.

PS 8 **(i)** Work out the area of quadrilateral ABCD.

   (ii) Work out the length of diagonal BD.

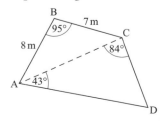

Exercise 7.5 Problems in three dimensions

Where necessary, leave answers approximated to 1 decimal place.

1 AB = 12 cm, BC = 3 cm and CF = 4 cm are three sides of cuboid ABCDEFGH.

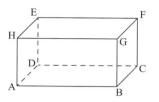

   (i) Work out length BD.

   (ii) Work out length HC.

   (iii) Work out angle CAF.

2 ABCDEF is a triangular prism.

AB = 17 cm, AF = 8 cm, BF = 18 cm and BC = 10 cm.

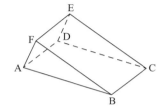

   (i) Work out angle ABF.

   (ii) Work out the angle between the planes ADEF and BCEF.

   (iii) Work out the area of triangle BDE.

3 ABCDE is a pyramid with a horizontal rectangular base ABCD.

Vertex E is vertically above the centre of the rectangle.

AB = 7 cm, BC = 4 cm and BE = 8 cm.

   (i) Work out the vertical height of the pyramid.

   (ii) Work out the angle between the line AE and the rectangle.

   (iii) Work out the angle between the plane ADE and the rectangle.

   (iv) Work out the angle between planes ABE and CDE.

PS **4** ABC is an equilateral triangle and is the horizontal base of a tetrahedron ABCD.

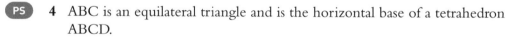

Vertex D is directly above vertex A.

Given that AB = AC = AD, calculate the angle between planes ABC and BCD.

PS **5** KLMNOPQR is a cube with sides of length 10 cm.

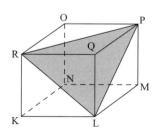

   (i) Work out the area of triangle LPR.

   (ii) Work out the acute angle between planes LPR and OPQR.

6 A box is in the shape of a cuboid with sides of length 12 cm, 9 cm and 5 cm.

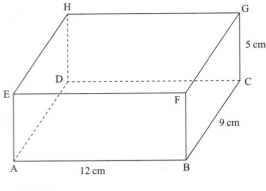

   (i)   Work out length AC.

   (ii) Work out the angle that line AG makes with the base ABCD.

   (iii) Work out length AF.

   (iv) Work out the angle that line AG makes with the front ABFE.

7 A wooden door wedge is in the shape of a triangular prism as shown.

   (i)   Work out length CE.

   (ii) Work out the volume of wood in the wedge.

   (iii) Work out the maximum number of such wedges that can be cut from a block of wood measuring 10 cm by 30 cm by 2 m.

8 A perfume bottle is made in the shape of a square-based pyramid, with the vertex directly above the centre of the base as shown.

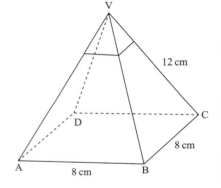

   (i)   Work out the angle between a slant edge and the base.

   (ii) Work out the angle between a side and the base.

9 A vase has a square base ABCD of side 10 cm and a square top EFGH of side 15 cm. The edges of one square are parallel to the edges of the other. The centres of the two squares are vertically aligned and 20 cm apart.

   (i)   Work out length AC.

   (ii) Work out length EG.

   (iii) Work out the length of the sloping edge AE.

   (iv) Work out the angle of inclination of a sloping edge to the horizontal.

10 A lean-to shed is used to store garden equipment and materials. The base of the shed is 2 m by 4 m, and the height is 2 m at the front and 3 m at the back.

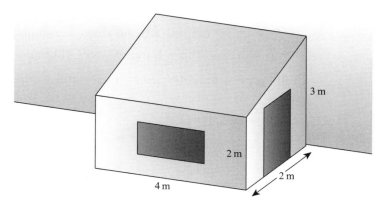

    (i) Work out the angle of inclination of the roof to the horizontal.

    (ii) Work out the volume of the shed.

    The door is 80 cm wide and 2 m high and is positioned in the middle of the end wall as shown. The window cannot be opened.

PS

    (iii) Work out the length of the longest metal rod that can be stored in the shed.

11 Linda is an advanced skier who is able to ski straight down a 100 m run on a slope inclined at 15° to the horizontal.

Tracey is a novice who can only ski down slopes inclined at 5°, so she needs to go across the slope as shown.

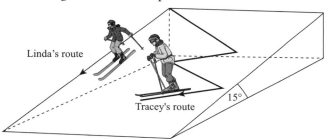

By considering the slope as a triangular prism, work out

    (i) the vertical fall of the 100 m run

PS

    (ii) the distance skied by Tracey in getting from the top to the bottom.

12 A swimming pool is in the shape of a prism with a trapezium cross-section. The surface of the water forms a rectangle ABCD with length 25 m and width 10 m.

The bottom of the pool is rectangle EFGH as shown.

The shallow end is 1 m deep.

The deepest end is 2.5 m deep.

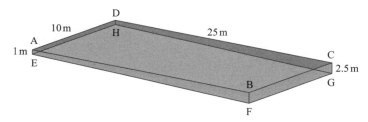

    (i) Work out length DF.

    (ii) Work out the angle of inclination of the bottom of the pool.

    (iii) Work out angle DHF.

If Ann-Marie stands on the bottom of the pool, then the water is above her chin if it is deeper than 1.4 m.

(iv) Work out the greatest horizontal distance she can stand from DH without the water being above her chin.

(v) Work out the volume of water in the pool.

13 Jim is presenting the news on television while seated at his desk in the studio.

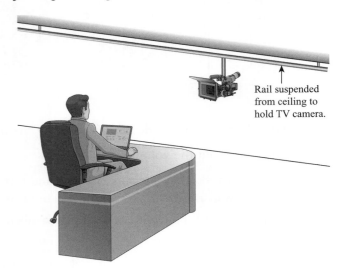

Rail suspended from ceiling to hold TV camera.

The camera runs on a horizontal track at a height of 2.2 m above the floor, and is 3 m horizontally from Jim at its closest. The camera track is 4 m long and Jim is seated opposite the centre of the track. Jim's eye level when seated is 1.25 m above the floor.

As the camera moves along the track, work out

(i) the least and greatest distances from it to Jim's eyes

(ii) the least and greatest angles of elevation of Jim's eyes if he looks directly at the camera.

PS **14** Anna is walking along a straight coastal path at sea level. From point A she records that the angle of elevation of the top of the lighthouse is 5°. After walking a further 200 m she reaches point B, from which the angle of elevation is 6°. The top of the lighthouse is 80 m above sea level.

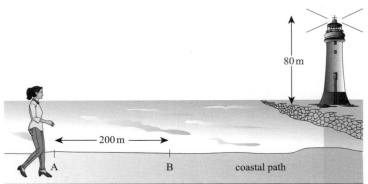

80 m

200 m

A   B   coastal path

(i) Work out the distances from each of points A and B to the centre of the lighthouse base.

(ii) Work out the shortest distance from the centre of the lighthouse base to the coastal path.

(iii) If Anna remains on the coastal path, work out the maximum angle of elevation of the top of the lighthouse.

8 Calculus

Exercise 8.1 Differentiation

1 Differentiate the following functions.

   (i) $y = 4x^3$ **(ii)** $y = 3x^2$ **(iii)** $y = 4x$

   (iv) $y = -6x^7$ **(v)** $y = -7x^6$ **(vi)** $y = 0$

   (vii) $y = \dfrac{1}{2}x^2$ **(viii)** $y = \dfrac{1}{3}x^3$ **(ix)** $y = \dfrac{1}{4}x^4$

2 Differentiate the following functions.

   (i) $y = 2x^3 + 3x^2$ **(ii)** $y = 3x^4 + 4x^3$ **(iii)** $y = 4x^5 + 5x^4$

   (iv) $y = 3x + 5$ **(v)** $y = 2x - 4$ **(vi)** $y = 5 - 4x$

   (vii) $y = 3x^3 + 2$ **(viii)** $y = 4x^4 + 4$ **(ix)** $y = 5x^5 + 5$

3 Differentiate the following functions.

   (i) $y = 2x^4 - 4x^2 - 8x + 8$

   (ii) $y = 3x^4 - 4x^3 + 12x - 12$

   (iii) $y = 2x^5 + 5x^2 - 10x + 25$

4 Write down the rate of change of the following functions with respect to x.

   (i) $y = x - \dfrac{2}{x}$ **(ii)** $y = \dfrac{x^2}{2} - \dfrac{2}{x^2}$ **(iii)** $y = \dfrac{x^3}{3} - \dfrac{3}{x^3}$

   (iv) $y = x^3 - x^{-3}$ **(v)** $y = 2x^4 - 4x^{-2}$ **(vi)** $y = 4x^5 + 5x^{-4}$

5 Differentiate the following functions.

   (i) $y = 4x^3 - \dfrac{3}{x^4}$ **(ii)** $y = x - \dfrac{1}{x}$ **(iii)** $y = 2x^2 - \dfrac{1}{2x}$

   (iv) $y = \dfrac{3}{x^2} + \dfrac{2}{x^3}$ **(v)** $y = \dfrac{2}{5x^2} - \dfrac{5}{2x^5}$ **(vi)** $y = \dfrac{4}{x^3} - \dfrac{3}{x^4}$

6 A cuboid has sides of lengths $2x$, $3x$ and $4x$.

   (i) Work out the volume V and the surface area A of the cuboid in terms of x.

   (ii) Work out $\dfrac{\mathrm{d}V}{\mathrm{d}x}$ and $\dfrac{\mathrm{d}A}{\mathrm{d}x}$.

7 Work out the gradient of the curve $y = x^2 - 4x + 3$ at the points of intersection with

   (i) the x-axis

   (ii) the y-axis.

8 Work out the coordinates of the points on the curve $y = 2x^3 + 3x^2 - 12x - 9$ where the gradient is zero.

Exercise 8.2 Gradient functions and more complex differentiation

1 Work out the gradient function for the following functions.

(i) $y = x^2 (2x - 3)$ **(ii)** $y = 3x (2x^2 - 5)$

(iii) $y = (x - 2) (x + 5)$ **(iv)** $y = (x - 4) (x + 3)$

(v) $y = (2x - 1) (3x + 2)$ **(vi)** $y = (3x^2 - 2) (2x + 5)$

2 (i) Multiply out $(x - 3) (2x^2 + 5)$.

(ii) Use your answer to **(i)** to differentiate $y = (x - 3) (2x^2 + 5)$.

(iii) Leanne has written $y = (x - 3) (2x^2 + 5) \Rightarrow \dfrac{dy}{dx} = 1 \times 4x = 4x$.
What mistake has she made?

3 (i) Simplify $\dfrac{4x^3 + 2x}{x}$.

(ii) Use your answer to **(i)** to differentiate $y = \dfrac{4x^3 + 2x}{x}$.

4 Work out an expression for the rate of change of y with respect to x for each of the following.

(i) $y = \dfrac{2x^2 + 3x}{5}$ **(ii)** $y = \dfrac{2x^3 - 4x^2}{2x}$

(iii) $y = \dfrac{4x^3 - 3x^4}{x^2}$ **(iv)** $y = \dfrac{x^3}{3}(3x^2 + 2x - 3)$

(v) $y = x^{\frac{1}{2}}(3x^{\frac{3}{2}} + 4x^{\frac{5}{2}})$ **(vi)** $y = 2x^{\frac{3}{2}}(x^{\frac{1}{2}} - x^{-\frac{1}{2}})$

5 Work out the gradient of the curve $y = x^2 (2x - 1)$ at the following points.

(i) $(0, 0)$ **(ii)** $(-1, -3)$ **(iii)** $(2, 12)$

6 Work out the gradient of the following curves at the point where $x = 2$.

(i) $y = x^2 - 3x$ **(ii)** $y = x^2 - 6x + 10$ **(iii)** $y = 3x^4 - 2x + 4$

7 Work out the gradient of the following curves at the point where $x = -3$.

(i) $y = 3x^3 - 2x + 4$ **(ii)** $y = \dfrac{1}{2}x^2 - 3x - 1$ **(iii)** $y = \dfrac{2}{3}x^3 + \dfrac{3}{2}x^2$

8 Work out the rate of change of y with respect to x for the curve
$y = \dfrac{2x^2 - 3x^3}{x}$ at the point $(-1, -5)$.

9 Work out the gradient of the curve $y = 2x\sqrt{x} + \dfrac{2}{\sqrt{x}}$ at the point $(1, 4)$.

10 Work out the coordinates of the points on the curve $y = 2x^3 - 3x^2 - 36x + 10$ where the gradient is zero.

11 A curve has equation $y = (x + 2) (x - 1) (x - 4)$. Work out the gradient of the curve at the points of intersection with the x and y axes.

Exercise 8.3 Tangents and normal

1 The sketch shows the graph of $y = x^2 - 4$.

The marked point, P, has coordinates $(1, -3)$.
Work out

   (i) the gradient function $\dfrac{dy}{dx}$

   (ii) the gradient of the curve at P

   (iii) the equation of the tangent at P

   (iv) the equation of the normal at P.

2 The sketch shows the graph of
$y = (x - 1)(x + 2)(x - 3)$.

Multiply out the brackets and hence work out

   (i) the gradient function $\dfrac{dy}{dx}$

   (ii) the gradient of the curve at each of the points where it crosses the x-axis

   (iii) the equation of the tangent at the point $(2, -4)$

   (iv) the equation of the normal at the point $(2, -4)$.

3 **(i)** Sketch the curve $y = x^2 - 4x$.

   (ii) Show that the point $(5, 5)$ lies on the curve and work out the gradient of the curve at this point.

4 The sketch shows the curve $y = x^3 - 6x^2 + 11x - 6$.

   (i) Differentiate $y = x^3 - 6x^2 + 11x - 6$.

   (ii) Show that the tangents at two of the points where the curve cuts the x-axis are parallel.

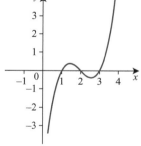

5 The sketch shows the curves with equations $y = x^2 - 4$ and $y = 4 - x^2$ for $-3 \leqslant x \leqslant 3$.

   (i) Work out the gradient of the curve $y = x^2 - 4$ at the points where $x = 1$ and $x = -1$.

   (ii) Work out the gradient of the curve $y = 4 - x^2$ at the points where $x = 1$ and $x = -1$.

   (iii) Write the equations of the tangents to the curves at those four points.

   (iv) Add the tangents to a copy of the graph and state the points of intersection of the tangents with the x-axis.

   (v) What type of quadrilateral is formed?

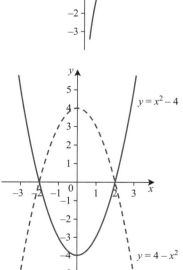

6 (i) Sketch, on the same axes, the curves with equations $y = x^2 - 6$ and $y = x^2 + 1$ for $-3 \leqslant x \leqslant 3$.

(ii) Work out the gradient of the curve $y = x^2 + 1$ at the point $(2, 5)$.

(iii) Give two explanations, one involving geometry and one involving calculus, to show why the gradient at the point $(2, -2)$ on the curve $y = x^2 - 6$ should have the same value as your answer to part **(ii)**.

(iv) Give the equation of another curve with the same gradient function as $y = x^2 + 1$.

7 $f(x) = ax^3 + 2x^2 + b$. The graph $y = f(x)$ goes through the point $(2, 0)$ with gradient -4.

(i) Using the fact that $(2, 0)$ lies on the curve, write an equation involving a and b.

(ii) Differentiate $f(x)$ and using the fact that the gradient is -4 at the point $(2, 0)$ form another equation.

(iii) Solve these equations simultaneously to work out the values of a and b.

(iv) Sketch the curve.

8 The sketch shows the curve with equation $y = x^4 + \dfrac{2}{x^2}$.

(i) Explain why the curve is symmetrical about the y-axis.

(ii) Work out the gradient function $\dfrac{dy}{dx}$ and calculate the coordinates of the minimum turning points.

(iii) State the equations of the tangent and normal at those points.

(iv) Work out the equations of the tangent and normal at the point $(2, 16.5)$.

(v) Deduce the equations of the tangent and normal at the point $(-2, 16.5)$.

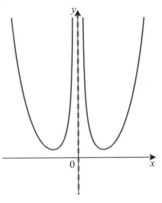

Exercise 8.4 Increasing and decreasing functions

1 Work out the values of x for which the following functions are increasing.

(i) $y = 2x^2 - 4$ **(ii)** $y = 3x - 4$

(iii) $y = x^2 - 4x + 5$ **(iv)** $y = x^2 + 5x$

(v) $y = 2x^2 - 4x + 3$ **(vi)** $y = (x + 2)(x - 4)$

(vii) $y = 2x^3 - 3x^2$ **(viii)** $y = 3x^3 - 6x + 5$

2 Work out the values of x for which the following functions are decreasing.

(i) $y = 3x^2 - 3$ **(ii)** $y = x^2 - 4x + 5$

(iii) $y = 2x(x - 4)$ **(iv)** $y = \dfrac{x}{2} - x^2$

(v) $y = (4 + x)(x - 3)$ **(vi)** $y = 5 - x^3$

(vii) $y = (2x - 3)^2$ **(viii)** $y = 6 + 3x - x^3$

3 Prove that $x^3 + 3x^2 + 6x - 4$ is an increasing function for all values of x.

4 Prove that $5 - 4x - x^3$ is a decreasing function for all values of x.

5 Work out the values of x for which the following functions are

        (a) increasing   **(b)** decreasing.

    (i) $y = 1 + 4x + \dfrac{1}{x}$

    (ii) $y = 2x^3 - 3x^2 - 36x + 9$

    (iii) $y = x^3 - x$

    (iv) $y = x^4 - 16$

6 Prove that $y = (x - a)^3$ is an increasing function for all values of a.

7 **(i)** Work out the values of x for which $y = x^3 - 15x^2 + 63x - 10$ is a decreasing function.

    (ii) Deduce the values of x for which it is an increasing function.

8 The population P of an endangered species has been monitored over a period of t years, where $0 \leqslant t \leqslant 6$, and it is thought that it follows the equation $P = 1000 - 4t - t^2$.

    (i) What was the value of P at the start of the survey?

    (ii) Work out, in terms of t, the rate of decrease of the population.

    (iii) By what percentage has the population decreased at the end of the survey?

9 The population P of a new town is modelled by the formula $P = t^3 - t^2 + 120t + 8000$, where t represents the number of years after the start of 2018. Use this formula to predict

    (i) the population at the start of 2025

    (ii) the rate of growth of the population at the start of 2025

    (iii) the year in which the population first exceeds $10\,000$.

Exercise 8.5 Second derivatives

1 Work out $\dfrac{dy}{dx}$ and $\dfrac{d^2y}{dx^2}$ for each of the following expressions.

    (i) $y = 2x^3 - 3x^2$ **(ii)** $y = 5x - 4$ **(iii)** $y = 4x - x^4$

2 Work out $\dfrac{dy}{dx}$ and $\dfrac{d^2y}{dx^2}$ for each of the following expressions.

    (i) $y = 2x^4 - 3x^2 - 5x + 2$

    (ii) $y = x^6 - 6x^2 + 3x + 1$

    (iii) $y = 2x^3 + 4x^2 - 7x - 2$

3 Work out $\dfrac{dy}{dx}$ and $\dfrac{d^2y}{dx^2}$ for each of the following expressions. Remember that when an expression involves brackets you need to multiply out before differentiating.

    (i) $y = (2x - 3)(3x - 2)$

    (ii) $y = (x^2 - 1)(x + 1)$

    (iii) $y = (4x - 3)^3$

4 Work out $\dfrac{\mathrm{d}y}{\mathrm{d}x}$ and $\dfrac{\mathrm{d}^2y}{\mathrm{d}x^2}$ for each of the following expressions.

    (i) $\quad y = 5\,(4x - 1)\,(x^2 + 2)$

    (ii) $\quad y = 3x\,(2x - 5)\,(2x + 3)$

    (iii) $y = 5x\,(3x - 2)^2$

5 The sum of two numbers, x and y, is 20 and their product, P, is 96.

    (i) Write down an expression for y in terms of x.

    (ii) Write down an expression for P in terms of x.

    (iii) Write down expressions for $\dfrac{\mathrm{d}y}{\mathrm{d}x}$ and $\dfrac{\mathrm{d}P}{\mathrm{d}x}$.

    (iv) Write down the rate of change of $\dfrac{\mathrm{d}P}{\mathrm{d}x}$.

6 For the curve $y = (x - 3)\,(2x^2 + 3x - 4)$

    (i) work out expressions for $\dfrac{\mathrm{d}y}{\mathrm{d}x}$ and $\dfrac{\mathrm{d}^2y}{\mathrm{d}x^2}$

    (ii) work out the gradient of the curve at the points $(-2, 10)$, $(0, 12)$ and $(3, 0)$

    (iii) use the information in **(ii)** to sketch the curve.

7 A stone is projected vertically upwards with a speed of $15\,\mathrm{m\,s^{-1}}$. After t seconds its height, h, is given by $h = 15t - 5t^2$.

    (i) Work out $\dfrac{\mathrm{d}h}{\mathrm{d}t}$ and $\dfrac{\mathrm{d}^2h}{\mathrm{d}t^2}$.

    (ii) Describe what is happening when $\dfrac{\mathrm{d}h}{\mathrm{d}t} = 0$.

    (iii) Sketch the graph of h against t.

8 The curve $y = x^4 - 9x^2$ meets the x-axis at three points.

    (i) Work out the gradient of the curve at each of these three points.

    (ii) Sketch the curve and add the tangents at each of the three points in **(i)** to your diagram.

    (iii) Work out the equations of these three tangents and work out their points of intersection.

    (iv) Calculate the area of the triangle whose vertices are the three points of intersection.

Exercise 8.6 Stationary points and applications of maxima and minima

If you have access to a graphics calculator you will find it helpful to use it to check your answers.

1 For each of the curves given on the next page

    (a) work out $\dfrac{\mathrm{d}y}{\mathrm{d}x}$ and the value(s) of x for which $\dfrac{\mathrm{d}y}{\mathrm{d}x} = 0$

    (b) work out the value(s) of $\dfrac{\mathrm{d}^2y}{\mathrm{d}x^2}$ at those points

(c) classify the point(s) on the curve with these x-values

(d) work out the corresponding y-value(s)

(e) sketch the curve.

(i) $y = x^2 - x - 2$

(ii) $y = 6 - 5x - 6x^2$

(iii) $y = x^3 - 3x$

(iv) $y = x^3 + 3x^2 - 24x - 7$

(v) $y = (x + 1)^2 (x - 1)^2$

2 The graph of $y = x^2 - ax + b$ has a minimum turning point at $(2, -3)$. Use this information to calculate the values of a and b.

3 A curve has equation $y = x^4 - 8x^2$.

(i) Work out $\dfrac{dy}{dx}$ and $\dfrac{d^2y}{dx^2}$.

(ii) Calculate the coordinates of any stationary points and work out their nature.

(iii) Sketch the curve.

4 A curve has equation $y = 4x^3 - 16x$.

(i) Work out $\dfrac{dy}{dx}$ and $\dfrac{d^2y}{dx^2}$.

(ii) Calculate the coordinates of any stationary points and work out their nature.

(iii) Sketch the curve.

5 A curve has equation $y = (x - 1)^2 (x - 4)$

(i) Work out $\dfrac{dy}{dx}$ and $\dfrac{d^2y}{dx^2}$.

(ii) Calculate the coordinates of any stationary points and work out their nature.

(iii) Sketch the curve.

6 The curve $y = ax^2 + bx + c$ crosses the y-axis at the point $(0, 3)$ and has a maximum point at $(1, 4)$.

(i) Work out the equation of the curve.

(ii) Confirm that the stationary point is a maximum.

7 The sum of two numbers x and y is 12.

(i) Write down an expression for y in terms of x.

(ii) Write down an expression for S, the sum of the squares of the two numbers, in terms of x.

(iii) Work out $\dfrac{dS}{dx}$ and $\dfrac{d^2S}{dx^2}$.

(iv) Work out the least value of S.

8 A cylindrical pencil holder (base but no top) is made from a thin sheet of metal. Its height is h cm and the radius of its base is r cm. The surface area is 250π cm^2.

    (i) Work out h in terms of r.

    (ii) Work out an expression for the volume, V, of the pencil holder in terms of r.

    (iii) Work out $\dfrac{\mathrm{d}V}{\mathrm{d}r}$ and $\dfrac{\mathrm{d}^2V}{\mathrm{d}r^2}$.

    (iv) Work out the dimensions of the pencil holder when the volume is a maximum.

9 An open box is to be made from a square sheet of cardboard, with sides 48 cm long, by cutting a square of side x cm from each corner, folding up the sides and joining the cut edges.

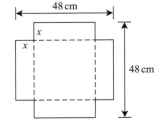

    (i) Write down an expression for the volume of the box.

    (ii) Work out the maximum capacity of the box.

10 A piece of wire 56 cm long is cut into two pieces. The shorter piece is $8x$ cm long and is bent to form a rectangle with sides $3x$ cm and x cm. The remaining piece is bent to form a square.

    (i) Work out, in terms of x, the dimensions of the square and its area.

    (ii) Show that the combined area of the square and the rectangle is A cm^2 where $A = 7x^2 - 56x + 196$.

    (iii) Work out the value of x for which A has its minimum value.

    (iv) Work out the minimum value of A.

11 An open box is to be made out of a rectangular piece of card measuring 120 cm by 75 cm. Squares of side x cm are cut from each corner of the card and the remaining card is folded to form the box.

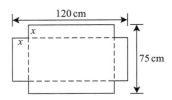

    (i) Work out an expression in terms of x for the volume of the box.

    (ii) Work out the value of x that gives the box the maximum possible volume.

    (iii) Calculate the maximum volume.

9 Matrices

Exercise 9.1 Multiplying matrices

1 $\mathbf{A} = \begin{bmatrix} 2 & -3 \\ 1 & 4 \end{bmatrix}$ and $\mathbf{B} = \begin{bmatrix} -5 & -1 \\ 3 & 6 \end{bmatrix}$

Work out:

(i) $2\mathbf{A} + \mathbf{B}$ (ii) $\mathbf{AB}$ (iii) $\mathbf{BA}$ (iv) $\mathbf{A}^2$

2 Solve the equations

(i) $\begin{bmatrix} p & 2 \\ 3 & 5 \end{bmatrix}\begin{bmatrix} -2 \\ 7 \end{bmatrix} = \begin{bmatrix} 3 \\ q \end{bmatrix}$ (ii) $\begin{bmatrix} n & 2 \\ -5 & 6 \end{bmatrix}\begin{bmatrix} 4 \\ m \end{bmatrix} = \begin{bmatrix} 3 \\ 8 \end{bmatrix}$

3 $\mathbf{C} = \begin{bmatrix} 5 & 3 \\ 3 & -4 \end{bmatrix}$ and $\mathbf{D} = \begin{bmatrix} 2 & 4 \\ 6 & -9 \end{bmatrix}$

Given that $r\mathbf{C} + t\mathbf{D} = \begin{bmatrix} m & 6 \\ 0 & n \end{bmatrix}$, work out the values of m, n, r and t.

4 Solve the equations

(i) $\begin{bmatrix} 3 & a \\ 0 & 2 \end{bmatrix}\begin{bmatrix} 1 \\ 4 \end{bmatrix} = \begin{bmatrix} 9 \\ 8 \end{bmatrix}$ (ii) $\begin{bmatrix} 3 & 1 \\ b & -3 \end{bmatrix}\begin{bmatrix} 7 \\ -1 \end{bmatrix} = \begin{bmatrix} 20 \\ 17 \end{bmatrix}$

5 Given that $\begin{bmatrix} 3 & 1 \\ 2 & -4 \end{bmatrix}\begin{bmatrix} x \\ y \end{bmatrix} = \begin{bmatrix} 13 \\ 18 \end{bmatrix}$

(i) write down two equations in x and y

(ii) hence work out the values of x and y.

6 Solve the equations

(i) $\begin{bmatrix} 2 & 3 \\ 10 & x \end{bmatrix}\begin{bmatrix} 1 & y \\ -4 & 5 \end{bmatrix} = \begin{bmatrix} -10 & -9 \\ x & w \end{bmatrix}$ (ii) $\begin{bmatrix} 5 & p \\ -4 & 2 \end{bmatrix}\begin{bmatrix} 3 & 4 \\ q & 6 \end{bmatrix} = \begin{bmatrix} 9 & -6 \\ r & -4 \end{bmatrix}$

7 Work out the value of m such that $m\begin{bmatrix} 1 \\ m \end{bmatrix} - 6\begin{bmatrix} 2 \\ -1 \end{bmatrix} = m\begin{bmatrix} -m \\ 5 \end{bmatrix}$.

8 $\mathbf{M} = \begin{bmatrix} p-1 & 4 \\ 0 & p-q \end{bmatrix}$, $\mathbf{N} = \begin{bmatrix} 2p-q & 1 \\ 2p & 5q \end{bmatrix}$

$p\mathbf{M} + \mathbf{N} = \begin{bmatrix} 10 & 3p+2q \\ 2p & 13 \end{bmatrix}$

(i) Write down three equations in p and q.

(ii) Hence work out the values of p and q.

9 $\mathbf{C} = \begin{bmatrix} 3 & 2 \\ -1 & n \end{bmatrix}$ and $\mathbf{D} = \begin{bmatrix} 3 & m \\ 1 & 0 \end{bmatrix}$

Solve $\mathbf{CD} = \mathbf{DC}$.

10 $\mathbf{A} = \begin{bmatrix} -5 & 4 \\ 6 & 1 \end{bmatrix}$ and $\mathbf{B} = \begin{bmatrix} a & b \\ c & 4 \end{bmatrix}$

Given that $\mathbf{AB} = \mathbf{BA}$ work out b and c in terms of a.

11 $\mathbf{A} = \begin{bmatrix} 2 & 1 \\ 5 & 3 \end{bmatrix}$, $\mathbf{B} = \begin{bmatrix} 7 & -3 \\ 0 & 4 \end{bmatrix}$ and $\mathbf{C} = \begin{bmatrix} -3 & 6 \\ 4 & 2 \end{bmatrix}$

(i) Calculate **AB**.

(ii) Calculate **BC**.

(iii) Hence show that $(\mathbf{AB})\mathbf{C} = \mathbf{A}(\mathbf{BC})$

PS **12** Given that $\begin{bmatrix} 2 & 3 \\ 1 & 2 \end{bmatrix}\begin{bmatrix} a & b \\ c & d \end{bmatrix} = \begin{bmatrix} 1 & 0 \\ 0 & 1 \end{bmatrix}$ work out the values of a, b, c and d.

PS **13** Work out matrix **M** such that $\mathbf{M}\begin{bmatrix} 4 & 3 \\ 3 & 2 \end{bmatrix} = \begin{bmatrix} 1 & 0 \\ 0 & 1 \end{bmatrix}$.

Exercise 9.2 Transformations and matrices

1 Work out the image of each of these points under the transformation defined by the matrix $\begin{bmatrix} 2 & 6 \\ -1 & 5 \end{bmatrix}$.

(i) $(3, 5)$

(ii) $(-2, 4)$

2 Work out, in terms of a and b, the image of the point (a, b) under the transformation defined by the matrix $\begin{bmatrix} -4 & 2 \\ 3 & 1 \end{bmatrix}$.

3 $(5, 2)$ is the image of the point $(1, 3)$ under the transformation defined by matrix **A**. Work out the value of a when **A** is:

(i) $\begin{bmatrix} a & 3 \\ 2 & 0 \end{bmatrix}$ (ii) $\begin{bmatrix} 4 & a \\ -1 & 1 \end{bmatrix}$ (iii) $\begin{bmatrix} 2 & 1 \\ -1 & a \end{bmatrix}$

4 $(3, 4)$ is the image of the point $(1, 2)$ under the transformation defined by the matrix $\begin{bmatrix} a & b \\ 2a & -b \end{bmatrix}$.

(i) Write down two equations in a and b.

(ii) Hence work out the values of a and b.

5 For each equation work out matrix **M**.

(i) $\begin{bmatrix} 3 & 7 \\ 2 & -5 \end{bmatrix} + \mathbf{M} = \mathbf{I}$

(ii) $\mathbf{M} - \begin{bmatrix} 6 & -3 \\ 1 & 0 \end{bmatrix} = 2\mathbf{I}$

(iii) $2\mathbf{M} - 3\mathbf{I} = \begin{bmatrix} 5 & 0 \\ 4 & 1 \end{bmatrix}$

6 Work out matrix **M** such that $\mathbf{MI} + \mathbf{I}^2 = \begin{bmatrix} 4 & -1 \\ 3 & 6 \end{bmatrix}$.

7 Solve

(i) $\begin{bmatrix} 3 & 7 \\ 2 & 4 \end{bmatrix}\begin{bmatrix} -4 & c \\ 2 & -3 \end{bmatrix} = 2\mathbf{I}$ (ii) $\begin{bmatrix} d & -7 \\ -3 & e \end{bmatrix}\begin{bmatrix} 5 & 7 \\ 3 & 4 \end{bmatrix} = -1\mathbf{I}$

8   Point D is transformed under matrix **B** to the point $(4, 2)$.
    Work out the coordinates of point D when **B** is:

(i) $\begin{bmatrix} 2 & 1 \\ -4 & 3 \end{bmatrix}$
(ii) $\begin{bmatrix} 1 & 2 \\ 4 & 9 \end{bmatrix}$

PS 9 Show that the origin does not move when transformed using the

matrix $\begin{bmatrix} a & b \\ c & d \end{bmatrix}$.

PS 10 The point (x, y) does not move under the transformation defined by the

matrix $\begin{bmatrix} 2 & 3 \\ 0 & 1 \end{bmatrix}$.

(i) Write an equation connecting x and y.

(ii) Write down the coordinates of any point, other than $(0, 0)$, which does

not move under the transformation $\begin{bmatrix} 2 & 3 \\ 0 & 1 \end{bmatrix}$.

Exercise 9.3 Transformations of the unit square

1   Write down the matrices that represent the following reflections.

(i)   reflection in the line $x = 0$

(ii) reflection in the $y = 0$

(iii) reflection in the line $x - y = 0$

(iv) reflection in the line $x + y = 0$

2   Write down the matrices that represent the following rotations.

(i)   rotation of 90° about the origin

(ii) clockwise rotation of 90° about the origin

(iii) rotation of 180° about the origin

3   Write down the matrices that represent the following enlargements.

(i)   enlargement, scale factor 7, centre at the origin

(ii) enlargement, scale factor $\frac{1}{3}$, centre at the origin

(iii) enlargement, scale factor -4, centre at the origin

4   Describe fully the transformations defined by the following matrices.

(i) $\begin{bmatrix} 3 & 0 \\ 0 & 3 \end{bmatrix}$
(ii) $\begin{bmatrix} 0 & 1 \\ 1 & 0 \end{bmatrix}$
(iii) $\begin{bmatrix} 0 & -1 \\ 1 & 0 \end{bmatrix}$

(iv) $\begin{bmatrix} -1 & 0 \\ 0 & -1 \end{bmatrix}$
(v) $\begin{bmatrix} 0 & 1 \\ -1 & 0 \end{bmatrix}$
(vi) $\begin{bmatrix} -1 & 0 \\ 0 & 1 \end{bmatrix}$

5   The unit square has vertices $O(0, 0), A(1, 0), B(1, 1)$ and $C(0, 1)$.

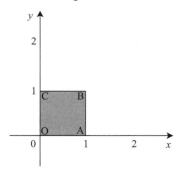

Write down the matrices that transform the unit square to the positions shown.

(i)

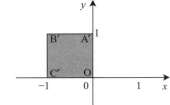

(ii)

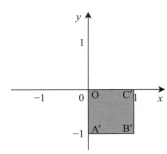

(iii)

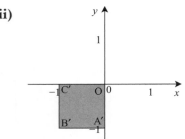

(iv)

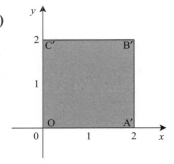

6 A square of area 1 is transformed under the matrix $\begin{bmatrix} 6 & 0 \\ 0 & 6 \end{bmatrix}$.

Work out the area of the transformed shape.

7 A square of area 1 is transformed under the matrix $\begin{bmatrix} a & 0 \\ 0 & a \end{bmatrix}$.

Work out the area of the transformed shape in terms of a.

8 The unit square has vertices O (0,0), P (1,0), Q (1,1) and R (0,1).
O, P′, Q′ and R′ are the images of O, P, Q and R, respectively, under the

transformation defined by the matrix $\begin{bmatrix} a & b \\ c & d \end{bmatrix}$.

(i) Work out the coordinates of P′, Q′ and R′ in terms of a, b, c and d.

(ii) Write down the vector $\overrightarrow{P'Q'}$ in terms of a, b, c and d.

(iii) Hence, or otherwise, prove that OP′Q′R′ is a parallelogram.

Exercise 9.4 Combining transformations

1 The point (1, 3) is transformed by $\begin{bmatrix} 3 & 1 \\ 2 & 0 \end{bmatrix}$ followed by a further

transformation $\begin{bmatrix} -2 & 4 \\ 3 & -5 \end{bmatrix}$.

(i) Work out the matrix for the combined transformation.

(ii) Hence work out the coordinates of the point after the two transformations.

2 **(i)** Write down the matrix that describes a reflection in the line $y = x$.

   (ii) Write down the matrix that describes a reflection in the x-axis.

   (iii) Hence work out the matrix that describes the combined transformation of a reflection in the line $y = x$, followed by a reflection in the x-axis.

   (iv) Describe geometrically the combined transformation in part **(iii)**.

3 The point $(4, -2)$ is rotated $90°$ clockwise about the origin, followed by a reflection in the y-axis.

   (i) Work out the matrix for the combined transformation.

   (ii) Hence work out the coordinates of the point $(4, -2)$ after the two transformations.

4 A unit square is enlarged by scale factor -7, centre the origin.

   (i) Write down the enlargement matrix.

   The enlarged shape is reflected in the line $x + y = 0$.

   (ii) Write down the reflection matrix.

   (iii) Hence work out the matrix for the combined transformation.

   (iv) Work out the area of the final transformed shape.

5 The point $(2, -1)$ is transformed by $\begin{bmatrix} 2 & 5 \\ -3 & 4 \end{bmatrix}$ followed by a further transformation $\begin{bmatrix} 1 & 7 \\ 0 & 3 \end{bmatrix}$.
   The new point is then transformed by $\begin{bmatrix} 3 & 6 \\ -2 & 4 \end{bmatrix}$.

   (i) Work out the matrix for the combination of the three transformations.

   (ii) Hence work out the new coordinates of the point $(2, -1)$ after the three transformations.

PS 6 **(i)** Work out the combined transformation matrix of $\begin{bmatrix} 4 & 7 \\ 1 & 2 \end{bmatrix}$ followed by $\begin{bmatrix} 2 & -6 \\ 3 & 4 \end{bmatrix}$ and then $\begin{bmatrix} -5 & 0 \\ 2 & 3 \end{bmatrix}$.

   (ii) Under this combined transformation, point A is mapped to the point $(-50, 377)$.
   Work out the coordinates of point A.

7 Use matrices to prove that a reflection in the line $y = -x$, followed by a reflection in the x-axis, is equivalent to a rotation of $90°$ about the origin.

PS 8 Transformation matrix **A** is a rotation.
   Given that $\mathbf{A}^2 = \mathbf{I}$, write down the rotation matrix **A**.

PS 9 Transformation matrix **B** is an enlargement scale factor k.
   Given that $\mathbf{BC} = \mathbf{I}$, write down the matrix **C**.

PS 10 Transformation matrix **D** is a reflection.
   Write down the matrix $\mathbf{D}^2$.

9

Chapter 9 Matrices

71

Answers

1 Number and algebra I

Exercise 1.1 Numbers and the number system

1 1.998 kg

2 £23.12

3 (i) 23 : 15   (ii) $1 : \frac{15}{23}$

4 10 : 3

5 £22.27

6 $\frac{41}{140}$

7 (i) $\frac{13}{18}$ (ii) 72.2%

8 (i) 60%   (ii) 7

Exercise 1.2 Simplifying expressions

1 (i) $2x^2 + xy$ (ii) $6p^2 - 15pq - 35q^2$

2 (i) $xy(x - y)$ (ii) $2pq^2(4p^2 - 3q^3)$

3 (i) $2a(a + 1)$ (ii) $p(p + 4)$

4 (i) $6a^3b^4$ (ii) $30x^4y^6z$

5 (i) $\frac{3}{4mn^3}$ (ii) $\frac{3y^2}{20x^5}$

6 (i) $\frac{2q + 5p}{pq}$ (ii) $\frac{x^2 + 1}{3x}$

7 $\frac{13x}{3y}$

8 (i) $14p - 8$ (ii) $6p^2 - p + 1$

Exercise 1.3 Solving linear equations

1 (i) $x = -8$ (ii) $y = 5$

2 (i) $x = 3.8$ (ii) $x = -2.5$

3 (i) $17°$ (ii) scalene

4 $p = 8.4$

5 (i) $4w + 40 = 320$ (ii) $6300 \, \text{m}^2$

6 $x = 6.75$

7 (i) 60   (ii) $x = -\frac{380}{13}$

8 36

Exercise 1.4 Algebra and number

1 (i) $3m = 8n$ (ii) 37.5%

2 (i) $24 \times \frac{100 + a}{100} = b \times \frac{100 - 24}{100}$

   (ii) $19b - 6a = 600$

3 12

4 20

5 20

6 (i) $0.8h$ (ii) 5 : 6   (iii) £175

7 (i) 1 : 14   (ii) z is 47.6% of x

8 p is 71.4% of m

Exercise 1.5 Expanding brackets

1 (i) $x^2 + 3x + 2$ (ii) $2x^2 - x - 15$

2 (i) $m^3 + 1$ (ii) $x^5 - 1$

3 (i) $x^3 + 3x^2 - x - 3$ (ii) $6y^3 - 37y^2 + 32y + 15$

4 (i) $-2x - 10$ (ii) $m^2 - 8m - 3$

5 $a = 4, b = 1$

6 (i) $9m^2 - 6m + 1$

   (ii) $27m^3 - 27m^2 + 9m - 1$

7 (i) (a) $x^5 + 5x^3 - 2x^2 - 10$

      (b) $x^4 - 7x^3 + 3x - 21$

   (ii) $x^5 - x^4 + 12x^3 - 2x^2 - 3x + 11$

8 (i) $2x^3 - x^2 - 5x - 2$ (ii) $10x^2 - 2x - 6$

Exercise 1.6 Binomial expansions – using Pascal's triangle only

1 $x^3 + 6x^2 + 12x + 8$

2 $16x^4 + 32x^3y + 24x^2y^2 + 8xy^3 + y^4$

3 (i) $a^5 + 5a^4b + 10a^3b^2 + 10a^2b^3 + 5ab^4 + b^5$

   (ii) $32x^5 - 240x^4y + 720x^3y^2 - 1080x^2y^3 + 810xy^4 - 243y^5$

4 (i) 1, 13, 78

   (ii) $8192 + 53\,248x + 159\,744x^2$

5 4860

6 560

7 (i) 5   (ii) 2   (iii) 40

8 $-1\,959\,552$

Exercise 1.7 Surds: simplifying expressions containing square roots

1 (i) $6\sqrt{2}$ and $5\sqrt{2}$ (ii) $11\sqrt{2}$ (iii) $\sqrt{242}$

2 (i) $\dfrac{\sqrt{2}}{2}$ (ii) $3\sqrt{2}$ (iii) $\dfrac{5\sqrt{3}}{3}$

  (iv) $\dfrac{\sqrt{14}}{2}$ (v) $\sqrt{3}$ (vi) $\dfrac{2\sqrt{10}}{5}$

3 $\dfrac{11\sqrt{2}}{4}$

4 $x = \dfrac{7}{6}$

5 (i) $0 + \sqrt{8}$ (ii) $8 - \sqrt{12}$

  (iii) $5 + \sqrt{8}$ (iv) $\dfrac{4}{7} + \sqrt{\dfrac{32}{49}}$

6 (i) $16\,\text{cm}$ (ii) $14\,\text{cm}^2$ (iii) $6\,\text{cm}$

7 (i) $a^4 + 4a^3b + 6a^2b^2 + 4ab^3 + b^4$

  (ii) $193 + 132\sqrt{2}$

8 (i) $x = 1$

  (ii) $w = \dfrac{1}{4}(1 + 10\sqrt{3})$

  (iii) $y = 4$

  (iv) $m = \dfrac{8}{3}$

9 $x = \pm\sqrt{2}$

Exercise 1.8 Surds: rationalising denominators with two terms

1 (i) $2\sqrt{2} + 2$ (ii) $\dfrac{35 - 5\sqrt{3}}{46}$

  (iii) $\dfrac{3\sqrt{5} - 5}{4}$ (iv) $\dfrac{10\sqrt{6} + 12}{19}$

  (v) $\dfrac{9\sqrt{7} + 14}{53}$ (vi) $\dfrac{11 + 6\sqrt{2}}{7}$

  (vii) $\dfrac{23 - 9\sqrt{3}}{13}$ (viii) $\dfrac{102 + 32\sqrt{10}}{41}$

2 (i) $\dfrac{2}{23} + \dfrac{5}{23}\sqrt{2}$ (ii) $\dfrac{51}{47} + \dfrac{14}{47}\sqrt{2}$

  (iii) $8 + 7\sqrt{2}$ (iv) $-16 + \dfrac{23}{2}\sqrt{2}$

3 (i) $1 + \sqrt{3}$ (ii) $5 + \sqrt{50}$

  (iii) $\dfrac{6}{11} + \sqrt{\dfrac{3}{121}}$ (iv) $\dfrac{13}{11} + \sqrt{\dfrac{180}{121}}$

4 (i) 3 (ii) $\dfrac{7 + 2\sqrt{10}}{3}$

5 $\left(4 + \sqrt{2}\right)\text{cm}$

6 (i) $\left(13 - \sqrt{2}\right)\text{cm}$ (ii) $\left(8 + 2\sqrt{2}\right)\text{cm}$

7 (i) $2\sqrt{2}$

  (ii) $\dfrac{5\sqrt{6} - 12 - 2\sqrt{3} + 7\sqrt{2}}{4}$

  (iii) $\dfrac{3\sqrt{5} + 6\sqrt{15} - 9\sqrt{3} + 12}{22}$

8 $7\sqrt{2} + 4\sqrt{5} - 3\sqrt{10} - 9$

Exercise 1.9 The product rule for counting

1 720

2 (i) 6 (ii) 18

3 (i) $10\,000$ (ii) 5040

4 20

5 (i) $40\,320$ (ii) $1\,814\,400$

6 (i) $17\,496$ (ii) $20\,634$

7 (i) 6 (ii) 6 (iii) 42

8 (i) 6720 (ii) $32\,768$

2 Algebra II

Exercise 2.1 Factorising

1 (i) $(a + c)(b + c)$ (ii) $(p + q)(p + r)$

  (iii) $(a + c)(a + b)$

2 (i) $(a - 2b)(2b + 3c)$ (ii) $(2r - 3t)(r + 3s)$

  (iii) $(g - 2k)(3g - h)$

3 (i) $(x + 2)(x + 3)$ (ii) $(x - 2)(x - 5)$

  (iii) $(x - 5)(x + 2)$ (iv) $(p + 2)(p + 7)$

  (v) $(r - 3)(r - 12)$ (vi) $(t - 15)(t + 5)$

4 (i) $(2a + 1)(a + 2)$ (ii) $(2x + 3)(x - 2)$

  (iii) $(3p + 1)(p - 3)$ (iv) $(2a - 5)(a - 4)$

  (v) $(4c + 9)(c - 2)$ (vi) $(3x - 2)(x + 4)$

5 (i) $(x + 2y)(x + 4y)$ (ii) $(r + 5a)(r - 3a)$

  (iii) $(y + 4z)(y + 5z)$ (iv) $(a - 6b)(a + b)$

(v) $(p + 3q)(p + 4q)$

(vi) $(s - 2t)(s - 2t) = (s - 2t)^2$

6 (i) $(2x + 3y)(x + y)$

(ii) $(2a - b)(a - 2b)$

(iii) $(3p - q)(3p - q) = (3p - q)^2$

(iv) $(2x - y)(x - 5y)$

(v) $(3a - b)(a - b)$

(vi) $(2p + 3q)(3p - 2q)$

7 (i) $(x + 2y)(x - 2y)$

(ii) $(a + b + 2)(a - b - 2)$

(iii) $(p + 3 + 2q)(p + 3 - 2q)$

(iv) $(s + 3t + 6)(s - 3t - 6)$

(v) $(x - 1 + 4y)(x - 1 - 4y)$

(vi) $(2x - 1 + y)(2x - 1 - y)$

8 (i) $x(x + 3)(x - 3)$

(ii) $a^2(a + 2)(a - 2)$

(iii) $4p(p + 2)(p - 2)$

(iv) $(3a + b)(a + 3b)$

(v) $8pq$

(vi) $(5x - y)(5y - x)$

Exercise 2.2 Rearranging mathematical formulae

1 $x = \pm\sqrt{r^2 - y^2}$

2 $h = \dfrac{2A}{b}$

3 $b = \dfrac{P}{2} - l \left(\text{or } \dfrac{P - 2l}{2} \right)$

4 $r = \sqrt[3]{\dfrac{3V}{4\pi}}$

5 $l = \dfrac{A - \pi r^2}{\pi r} \left(\text{or } \dfrac{A}{\pi r} - r \right)$

6 (i) $h = \dfrac{2A}{b + c}$

(ii) $b = \dfrac{2A - ch}{h} \left(\text{or } \dfrac{2A}{h} - c \right)$

7 (i) $h = \dfrac{V}{\pi r^2}$

(ii) $r = \sqrt{\dfrac{V}{\pi h}}$ (must be positive)

8 (i) $y = \dfrac{3V}{x^2}$ **(ii)** $x = \sqrt{\dfrac{3V}{y}}$

9 (i) $a = \dfrac{v^2 - u^2}{2s}$

(ii) $u = \pm\sqrt{v^2 - 2as}$ (can be in positive or negative direction)

10 (i) $h = \dfrac{2A}{(a + b)}$

(ii) $a = \dfrac{2A - bh}{h} \left(\text{or } \dfrac{2A}{h} - b \right)$

Exercise 2.3 Rearranging more general formulae and equations

1 $p = \dfrac{3q}{4q - 2}$

2 $t = \dfrac{2a + 3b}{4}$

3 $r = \dfrac{2p}{p + 2}$

4 $c = \dfrac{6b}{3b + 2}$

5 $d = \dfrac{2(a + 3b)}{(a + 4b)}$

6 $a = \dfrac{3(b + 1)}{2(1 - b)}$

7 $x = \dfrac{1 + y}{1 - 2y}$

8 $s = \dfrac{3a}{p - 2}$

9 $w = \dfrac{3x + 2}{x - 1}$

10 $p = \dfrac{2a(a - 3)}{(7 - 3a)}$

Exercise 2.4 Simplifying algebraic fractions

1 (i) $\dfrac{b}{2a}$ **(ii)** $\dfrac{4b^3}{3ac^2}$ **(iii)** $\dfrac{3x}{2y}$

2 (i) $\dfrac{x + 2}{2x + 1}$ **(ii)** $\dfrac{3}{x + 2}$ **(iii)** $\dfrac{x + 6}{2}$

3 (i) $\dfrac{2x + 3}{3x - 2}$ **(ii)** $\dfrac{x - 2}{x + 2}$ **(iii)** $\dfrac{2x - 3}{3x + 2}$

4 (i) $\dfrac{2(2x - 1)}{3(x + 1)}$ **(ii)** $\dfrac{3x - 1}{3(2x - 1)}$

(iii) $\dfrac{1}{x - 2}$ **(iv)** $\dfrac{x + 2}{(x - 3)(x + 3)}$

5 (i) $\dfrac{3}{8x}$ **(ii)** 1

(iii) $\dfrac{3x-2}{(x-3)(2x+3)}$ **(iv)** $\dfrac{(x+2)^2}{x(x-2)^2}$

6 (i) $\dfrac{25p}{12}$ **(ii)** $\dfrac{25}{12p}$ **(iii)** $\dfrac{16p^2+9}{12p}$

7 (i) $\dfrac{25a+18}{(4a+3)(3a+2)}$

(ii) $\dfrac{4a^2}{(2a+3)(2a-3)}$

(iii) $\dfrac{a^2+b^2}{(a+b)(a-b)}$

8 (i) $\dfrac{5x}{6}$

(ii) $\dfrac{7}{12x}$

(iii) $\dfrac{9x^2-4}{6x}$

9 (i) $\dfrac{p-10}{p(p+2)(p-2)}$

(ii) $\dfrac{2}{x-2}$

(iii) $\dfrac{3x-x^2}{(x+1)(x+2)(x+3)}$

$$\left(=\dfrac{x(3-x)}{(x+1)(x+2)(x+3)}\right)$$

10 (i) $\dfrac{3a^3+a^2+a+1}{a^3}$

(ii) $-\dfrac{x}{3}$

Exercise 2.5 Solving linear equations involving fractions

1 (i) $x=\dfrac{9}{16}$

(ii) $x=2$

(iii) $x=\dfrac{30}{13}=2\dfrac{4}{13}$

2 (i) $x=\dfrac{9}{8}=1\dfrac{1}{8}$ **(ii)** $x=15$ **(iii)** $x=6$

3 (i) $x=5\dfrac{2}{3}$ **(ii)** $x=6$ **(iii)** $x=7$

4 (i) $x=24$ **(ii)** $x=-9$ **(iii)** $x=2$

5 (i) $x=0.1$ **(ii)** $x=0.5$ **(iii)** $x=\dfrac{1}{6}$

6 (i) $x=\dfrac{1}{6}$ **(ii)** $x=1$ **(iii)** $x=-13$

7 (i) $x=1.5$ or $x=-1$

(ii) $x=2$

(iii) $x=\dfrac{1}{6}$ or $x=-1$

8 (i) $p=8$

(ii) $q=7$

(iii) $r=-\dfrac{1}{13}$

Exercise 2.6 Completing the square

1 $a=3, b=3$

2 $c=4, d=5$

3 $p=5, q=1$

4 $r=10, s=-2$

5 $a=12, b=3, c=5$

6 $p=2, q=3, r=5$

7 $a=4, b=2, c=2$

8 $p=-4, q=5, r=-2$

9 (i) $a=3, b=11$

(ii) $x=-3\pm\sqrt{y-11}$

10 (i) $p=4, q=-2, r=-5$

(ii) $x=2\pm\dfrac{\sqrt{y+5}}{2}$

3 Algebra III

Exercise 3.1 Function notation

1 (i) 0 **(ii)** 2 **(iii)** 4

(iv) 6 **(v)** 2 **(vi)** 6

2 (i) 18 **(ii)** 18

(iii) $-\dfrac{2}{3}$ **(iv)** $\dfrac{2}{3}$

3 (i) $x=1.5$ **(ii)** $x=\dfrac{2}{3}$

(iii) $x=-1$

4 (i) $x=-5$ **(ii)** $x=\dfrac{1}{5}$ (or 0.2)

(iii) $x=8$

5 (i) $x=1$ **(ii)** $x=-3$ or $x=1$

(iii) $x=1\dfrac{2}{3}$ or $x=1$

6 (i) $4x + 5$ **(ii)** $2x^2 - 4x + 5$

(iii) $4x^2 + 4x + 1$

7 (i) $8x^2 + 6x + 1$ **(ii)** $8x^2 - 6x + 1$

(iii) $32x^4 + 12x^2 + 1$

(iv) $8x^4 + 6x^2 + 1$

8 (i) 4   **(ii) (a)** $x = \pm 2$

(b) $x = \pm 4$

9 (i) $-\dfrac{4}{5}$ (or -0.8) **(ii) (a)** $x = 4$

(b) $x = 0$

10 (i) (a) $x = 1.5$ **(b)** $x = -4.5$

(ii) leads to a false equality

11 (i) $4(3x + 1)^2$ **(ii)** $(3x - 4)^2$

(iii) $9x^2(3x + 4)^2$

Exercise 3.2 Domain and range of a function

1 (i) $f(x) \leq 4$ **(ii)** $f(x) \leq 4$

(iii) $f(x) \leq 1$ **(iv)** $f(x) \leq 0$

2 (i) $f(x) \leq 1$ **(ii)** $f(x) \leq -3$

(iii) $f(x) \leq -7$ **(iv)** $f(x) \leq -11$

3 (i) $0 < f(x) < 1$ **(ii)** $-0.5 < f(x) < 0.5$

(iii) $4 < f(x) < 5$ **(iv)** $3.5 < f(x) < 4.5$

(v) $-4 \leq f(x) \leq 2$ **(vi)** $-1 \leq f(x) \leq 3$

4 (i) $0 \leq f(x) \leq 16$ **(ii)** $0 \leq f(x) \leq 16$

(iii) $-2 \leq f(x) \leq 62$ **(iv)** $-62 \leq f(x) \leq 66$

5 (i) Domain $-2 \leq x \leq 5$
Range $-1 \leq f(x) \leq 13$

(ii) Domain $-3 \leq x \leq 4$
Range $-5 \leq f(x) \leq 9$

(iii) Domain $-2 \leq x \leq 3$
Range $0 \leq x \leq 16$

(iv) Domain $-2 \leq x \leq 2$
Range $-7 \leq x \leq 9$

6 (i) $-\dfrac{1}{4} \leq x < 6$ **(ii)** $-\dfrac{1}{4} \leq x < 12$

(iii) $2\dfrac{3}{4} \leq x < 9$ **(iv)** $-4\dfrac{1}{4} \leq x < 2$

7 (i) $-8 < f(x) < 12$ **(ii)** $-16 < f(x) < 20$

(iii) $0 \leq f(x) < 9$ **(iv)** $-9 < f(x) < 3$

8 (i) $0 \leq f(x) \leq 64$ **(ii)** $-9 \leq f(x) \leq 16$

(iii) $-5 \leq f(x) \leq 11$ **(iv)** $-9 \leq f(x) \leq 7$

Exercise 3.3 Composite functions

1 $g(x) = 2 - x, f(x) = x^3$

2 (i) (a) $x^2 - 4$

(b) $x^2 - 4x + 2$

(ii) (a) 0

(b) -2

(iii) $x = 1.5$

3 (i) (a) $2(2 + x)$

(b) $2 + 2x$

(ii) (a) 8

(b) 6

(iii) $x = 2$

4 (i) $h(x) = 1 + x, g(x) = \sqrt{x}$

(ii) $h(x) = 1 - x, g(x) = x^2$

(iii) $h(x) = 1 + x, g(x) = \dfrac{1}{x}$

5 (i) $k(x) = 3x; h(x) = 1 + x; g(x) = \sqrt{x}$

(ii) $k(x) = 2x; h(x) = 1 - x; g(x) = x^3$

(iii) $k(x) = 4x; h(x) = 1 - x; g(x) = \dfrac{1}{x}$

6 (i) $h(x) = 4x; g(x) = \sin x$

(ii) $h(x) = x - 45°; g(x) = \cos x$

(iii) $h(x) = \tan x; g(x) = \dfrac{1}{2}x$

7 (i) $k(x) = 4x; h(x) = \tan x; g(x) = 3x$

(ii) $k(x) = x + 30°; h(x) = \sin x; g(x) = \dfrac{1}{2}x$

(iii) $k(x) = 3x; h(x) = \cos x; g(x) = \dfrac{2}{x}$

8 (i) $fg(x) = (ax - 2)^2, gf(x) = ax^2 - 2$

(ii) $x = 1$ or $x = 3, 1 < x < 3$

(iii) $x = 1.5$

(iv) See full worked solution online.

9 d e b a c (or possibly e b d a c)

Exercise 3.4 Graphs of linear functions

1 (i) 2   **(ii)** 0

(iii) 0.4   **(iv)** -2

(v) -2 **(vi)** 1.25

(vii) 0.75   **(viii)** -1

(ix) -1 **(x)** -2

2

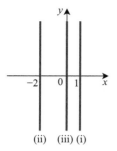

3

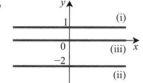

4

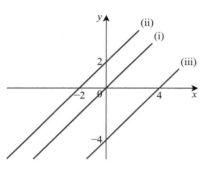

5

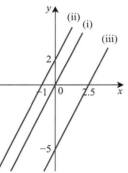

6

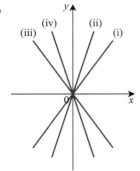

7

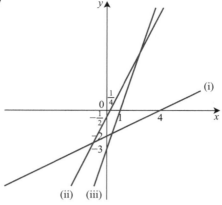

8

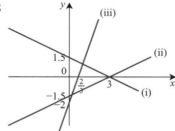

9

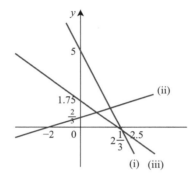

10

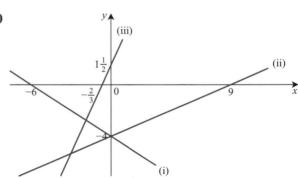

11 (i) $C = 50 + 25t$

(ii) £125

(iii) 8 hours

Exercise 3.5 Finding the equation of a line

1 (i) $y = 3$

   (ii) $y = -2x$ or $2x + y = 0$

   (iii) $y = -3x$ or $3x + y = 0$

   (iv) $x = -2$

2 (i) $y = 2 - x$ **(ii)** $y = 2 - 2x$

   (iii) $y = 2 - 3x$ **(iv)** $y = 3x + 2$

   (v) $y = 2x + 2$ **(vi)** $y = x + 2$

3 (i) $x + 2y = 3$ **(ii)** $x + y = 3$

   (iii) $2x + y = 3$ **(iv)** $2x - y = 3$

   (v) $x - 2y = 3$

4 (i) $y = x + 3$ **(ii)** $y = 2x + 5$

   (iii) $y = 3x - 10$ **(iv)** $y = 4x + 3$

5 (i) $y = 1 - x$

   (ii) $y = -2x - 5$ or $2x + y + 5 = 0$

   (iii) $y = -3x - 7$ or $3x + y + 7 = 0$

   (iv) $y = -4x + 20$ or $4x + y - 20 = 0$

6 (i) $x + y = 5$ **(ii)** $y = 4$

   (iii) $2x + y = 11$ **(iv)** $x + 3y = 19$

7 (i) $x + y = 1$ **(ii)** $y = -2x$

   (iii) $x + y + 3 = 0$ **(iv)** $x + y + 6 = 0$

8 (i)

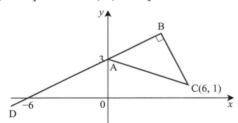

   (ii) AC $y = -\dfrac{1}{3}x + 3$

      BC $2x + y - 13 = 0$

   (iii) AB $= 2\sqrt{5}$, BC $= 2\sqrt{5}$, area $= 10$ units^2

9 (i) £21   **(ii)** £11.75

10 (i) £9.30   **(ii)** 10 miles

Exercise 3.6 Graphs of quadratic functions

1 (a) $y = 4x - x^2$ (eq^n (ii))

   (b) $y = x^2 - 2x + 3$ (eq^n (iv))

2 (a) $y = x^2 - 3x + 6$ (eq^n (i))

   (b) $y = x^2 - 6x + 6$ (eq^n (iv))

3 (a) $y = 4 - x^2$ (eq^n (i))

   (b) $y = -x^2 + 2x - 1$ (eq^n (iii))

4 (i) (a) Vertex $(1, -5)$

      (b) $x = 1$

      (c) $(0, -4)$

   (ii)

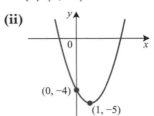

5 (i) (a) Vertex $(2, -2)$

      (b) $x = 2$

      (c) $(0, 2)$

   (ii)

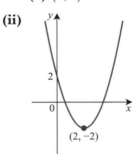

6 (i) (a) Vertex $(-1, -5)$

      (b) $x = -1$

      (c) $(0, -4)$

   (ii)

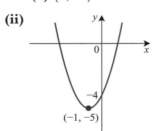

7 (i) (a) Vertex $(-1, -9)$

      (b) $x = -1$

      (c) $(0, -7)$

   (ii)

8 (i) $2(x - 0.5)^2 - 5.5$

    (a) Vertex $(0.5, -5.5)$

    (b) $x = 0.5$

    (c) $(0, -5)$

(ii)

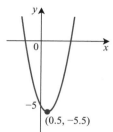

9 (i) $13 - (x - 3)^2$

    (a) Vertex $(3, 13)$

    (b) $x = 3$

    (c) $(0, 4)$

(ii)

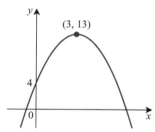

10 (i) $y = (x - 1)(x - 3)$

    (ii) $y = 3(x + 1)(x - 2)$

    (iii) $y = -x(x - 2)$

Exercise 3.7 Inverse functions

1 (i) $f^{-1}(x) = \dfrac{4x + 3}{2}$

    (ii)

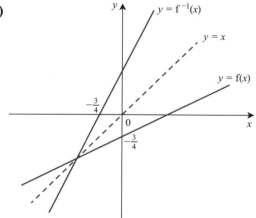

    (iii) $y = f(x)$ and $y = f^{-1}(x)$ are reflections in $y = x$

2 (i) $f^{-1}(x) = \dfrac{x - 2}{3}$

(ii)

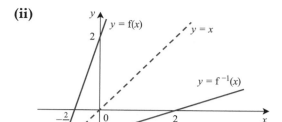

(iii) $ff^{-1}(3) = f\left(\dfrac{1}{3}\right) = 3$

    $f^{-1}f(3) = f^{-1}(11) = 3$

(iv) $ff^{-1}(x) = f^{-1}f(x)$

3 (i) $\dfrac{2 - 4x}{3}$

(ii)

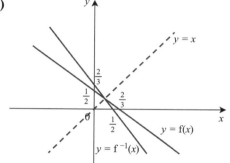

4 (i) $f^{-1}(x) = \sqrt{x + 9}\,; x \geqslant -9$

(ii)

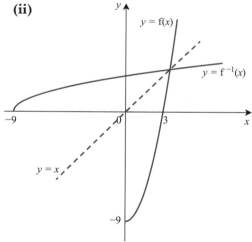

5 (i) $f^{-1}(x) = \sqrt{x} - 2\,; x \geqslant 0$

(ii)

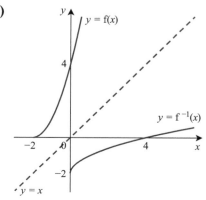

6 (i) $f^{-1}(x) = \left(\dfrac{x}{3}\right)^2 = \dfrac{x^2}{9}$; $x \geqslant 0$

(ii)

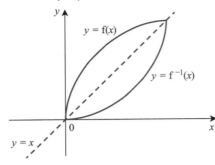

7 (i) $f^{-1}(x) = \dfrac{3}{x}$ for $x > 0$

(ii)

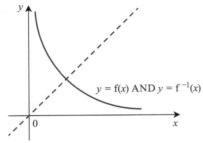

8 (i) $f^{-1}(-3) = -\dfrac{1}{3}$

(ii) $f^{-1}(-3) = 0$

(iii) $f^{-1}(-3) = -2\dfrac{1}{4}$

9 (i) $f^{-1}(8) = 2$

(ii) $f^{-1}(8) = 2\sqrt{2} - 4$

(iii) $f^{-1}(8) = \dfrac{\sqrt{11}}{2}$

10 (i) $f^{-1}(3) = \dfrac{3^2}{9} = 1$

(ii) $f^{-1}(3) = \dfrac{9}{3^2} = 1$

Exercise 3.8 Graphs of exponential functions

1

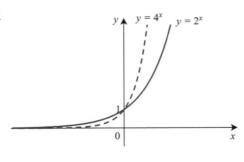

2

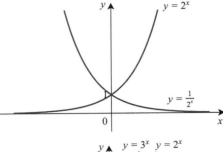

3

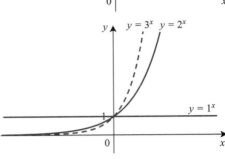

4

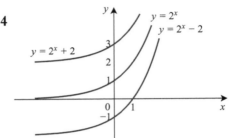

5

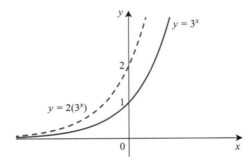

6 $y = 3^x \div 2$ and $y = 2^x \div 3$

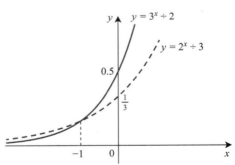

7 $y = 3^x \div 2$ and $y = (3 \div 2)^x$

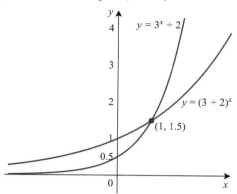

8 (i) $v = 25\,\text{ms}^{-1}$

(ii) $11\frac{2}{3}\,\text{ms}^{-1}$

(iii) $5.03\,\text{ms}^{-1}$ (2 d.p.)

(iv)

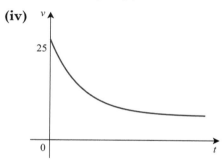

9 (i) 500

(ii) 574

(iii)

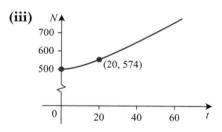

10 (i) 20 g

(ii) $t = 5 \Rightarrow m = 20 \times (0.5)^5 = 0.625$

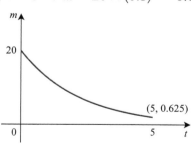

(iii) after 8 days

Exercise 3.9 Graphs of functions with up to three parts to their domains

1

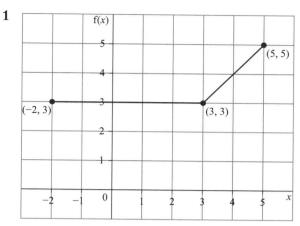

2

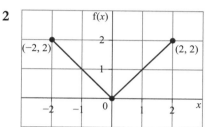

3

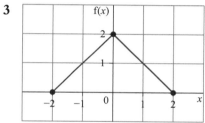

4

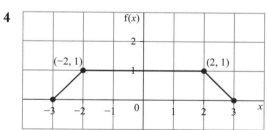

5

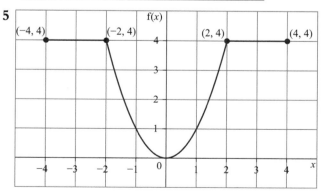

6

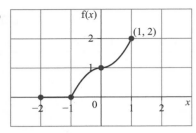

7 **(i)** $f(x) = x + 1$ $-1 \leqslant x \leqslant 0$
$\qquad\qquad = 1 - x$ $0 \leqslant x \leqslant 1$
$\qquad\qquad = 2x - 2$ $1 \leqslant x \leqslant 3$

(ii) $0 \leqslant f(x) \leqslant 4$

(iii) $x = 2$

8 **(i)** $f(x) = x + 2$ $-2 \leqslant x \leqslant 0$
$\qquad\qquad = 2$ $1 \leqslant x \leqslant 4$
$\qquad\qquad = 10 - 2x$ $4 \leqslant x \leqslant 5$

(ii) Range $0 \leqslant f(x) \leqslant 2$

(iii) 11 units^2

9 **(i)** $f(x) = 0$ $-4 \leqslant x \leqslant -2$
$\qquad\qquad = 4 - x^2$ $-2 \leqslant x \leqslant 2$
$\qquad\qquad = x - 2$ $2 \leqslant x \leqslant 4$

(ii) Range $0 \leqslant f(x) \leqslant 4$

(iii) 3

(iv) $x = -\sqrt{2}, \sqrt{2}, 4$

10 (i)

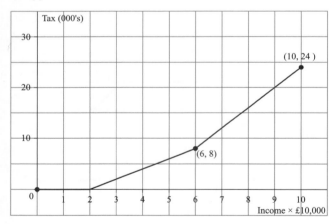

(ii) £3200

(iii) £14 000

(iv) Income = £80 000 pa

4 Algebra IV

Exercise 4.1 Solving quadratic equations by factorising, completing the square or using the quadratic formula

1 **(i)** $x = 2$ or 4 **(ii)** $y = 10$ or -1

(iii) $w = 6$ or -1 **(iv)** $p = 1.5$ or -5

(v) $n = -\dfrac{1}{3}$ or 7 **(vi)** $m = 3$ or $-\dfrac{1}{2}$

2 **(i)** $p = 3$ or 5 **(ii)** $x = 8$ or -2

(iii) $m = 1$ or -3 **(iv)** $t = \dfrac{3 \pm \sqrt{23}}{2}$

(v) $y = 5$ or 0.5 **(vi)** $n = \dfrac{2 \pm \sqrt{10}}{3}$

3 **(i)** $y = \dfrac{-5 \pm \sqrt{61}}{2}$ **(ii)** $p = \dfrac{3 \pm \sqrt{29}}{2}$

(iii) $m = -4 \pm \sqrt{14}$ **(iv)** $r = \dfrac{-3 \pm 3\sqrt{3}}{2}$

(v) $n = 1.4$ or -1 **(vi)** $w = \dfrac{-4 \pm \sqrt{22}}{3}$

4 **(i)** $x = 1.5$ or 4 **(ii)** $m = 11$ or 6

(iii) $a = \dfrac{11 \pm \sqrt{265}}{2}$

(iv) $y = 10.5$ or 3

(v) $n = 2$ or $\dfrac{3}{7}$ **(vi)** $p = -\dfrac{1}{3}$ or $-\dfrac{5}{4}$

5 **(i)** $x = \dfrac{5}{3}$ or 5 **(ii)** $w = -0.5$

(iii) $p = \dfrac{-11 \pm 3\sqrt{21}}{2}$

(iv) $y = \dfrac{-21 \pm \sqrt{473}}{2}$

(v) $t = \dfrac{8 \pm \sqrt{67}}{3}$

(vi) $a = -2$ or 2.2

6 **(i)** $2x + 1 > 2x$ and $2x + 1 > x + 1$

(ii) $6 \, \text{cm}^2$

7 $k = \dfrac{-1 \pm \sqrt{5}}{4} v$

8 $p = \dfrac{25}{12}$

Exercise 4.2 Solving simultaneous equations

1 **(i)** $x = 2, y = 2$ **(ii)** $q = -1, p = 5$

   (iii) $m = 2, n = 4$ **(iv)** $b = -1, a = 5$

   (v) $s = -3, r = 4$ **(vi)** $d = \frac{3}{13}, c = \frac{38}{13}$

2 **(i)** $x = 4, y = 5$ **(ii)** $x = 2, y = 10$

   (iii) $x = 1, y = 6$ **(iv)** $x = 5, y = -3$

   (v) $x = -1, y = 9$ **(vi)** $x = 5, y = -2$

3 **(i)** $x = 4, y = 7$ or $x = -2, y = 1$

   (ii) $x = 5, y = 3$ or $x = -1, y = -3$

   (iii) $x = 1, y = 1$ or $x = -2, y = -5$

   (iv) $x = -4, y = -3$

   (v) $x = 0.4, y = 2.2$ or $x = 2, y = -1$

   (vi) $x = -\frac{77}{17}, y = \frac{3}{17}$ or $x = 5, y = -3$

4 $\left(-\frac{58}{13}, -\frac{6}{13} \right)$ and $(2, 6)$

5 $\sqrt{192}$ cm

6 $2\sqrt{2}$

7 $a = -8, b = -18$

8 -33

Exercise 4.3 Factor theorem

1 and 2 See full worked solution online.

3 **(i)** See full worked solution online.

   (ii) $(x - 1)^2(x + 2)$

4 **(i)** 0

   (ii) $(x - 2)(x - 3)(x + 1)$

5 **(i)** See full worked solution online.

   (ii) $x = 3, 1 \pm \sqrt{2}$

6 -6

7 $(x + 5)$

8 $p = 10.5, q = 12.5$

Exercise 4.4 Linear inequalities

1 **(i)** $x > -\frac{2}{3}$ **(ii)** $x > -2$

   (iii) $x \geq \frac{5}{3}$ **(iv)** $x \geq 2.4$

(v) $x > 7.25$ **(vi)** $x \geq 10$

2 $-\frac{1}{2} < x \leq \frac{5}{3}$

3 **(i)** $x < 16$ **(ii)** $x \leq -21$

   (iii) $x \leq 3.5$ **(iv)** $x > -2$

   (v) $x < 1$ **(vi)** $x \leq 0.5$

4 **(i)** $-1 \leq x \leq 2$ **(ii)** $1 < x \leq 3$

   (iii) $-6 < x < 3$ **(iv)** $-3 < x \leq 2$

   (v) $17 < x \leq 22$ **(vi)** $0 \leq x < 40$

5 **(i)** $3 \leq p + q \leq 10$

   (ii) $-6 \leq p - q \leq 1$

   (iii) $4 \leq 2p + q \leq 13$

   (iv) $-20 \leq p - 3q \leq -3$

6 **(i)** $0 \leq m^2 \leq 16$

   (ii) $-6 \leq m + n < 8$

   (iii) $-25 < m^2 - n^2 \leq 16$

   (iv) $-8 \leq n^3 < 125$

7 **(i)** NEVER TRUE

   (ii) SOMETIMES TRUE

   (iii) ALWAYS TRUE

   (iv) ALWAYS TRUE

   (v) ALWAYS TRUE

   (vi) SOMETIMES TRUE

8 **(i)** SOMETIMES TRUE

   (ii) SOMETIMES TRUE

   (iii) SOMETIMES TRUE

   (iv) NEVER TRUE

   (v) ALWAYS TRUE

   (vi) SOMETIMES TRUE

Exercise 4.5 Quadratic inequalities

1 **(i)** $x < 1$ or $x > 3$ **(ii)** $-6 \leq x \leq -1$

   (iii) $x \leq -1$ or $x \geq 4$ **(iv)** $-2 \leq x \leq 7$

   (v) $1 < x < 7$ **(vi)** $-10 < x < 8$

2 **(i)** $x \leq -\frac{1}{4}$ or $x \geq 1$

   (ii) $-\frac{1}{2} < x < 1$

(iii) $-1 < x < \dfrac{3}{2}$ **(iv)** $x \leqslant \dfrac{1}{3}$ or $x \geqslant 2$

(v) $x < \dfrac{-3 - \sqrt{37}}{2}$ or $x > \dfrac{-3 + \sqrt{37}}{2}$

(vi) $-\dfrac{3}{2} \leqslant x \leqslant 3$

3 (i) $1 < x < 2$ **(ii)** $-1 < x < 1$

(iii) $\dfrac{1}{2} < x < 1$ **(iv)** $x < -3$ or $x > 3$

(v) $x < -\dfrac{3}{5}$ or $x > 1$

(vi) $x < \dfrac{1 - \sqrt{33}}{8}$ or $x > \dfrac{1 + \sqrt{33}}{8}$

4 $2 < x < \dfrac{11 + \sqrt{129}}{4}$

5 (i) $y > -9$ **(ii)** $y \leqslant -2$ or $y \geqslant 2$

(iii) $-9 < y \leqslant -2$ or $y \geqslant 2$

6 (i) $-4 < x < 2$ **(ii)** $-1 \leqslant x \leqslant 5$

(iii) $-1 \leqslant x < 2$

7 (i) $1 \leqslant x \leqslant 3$ **(ii)** $2 < y < 4$

(iii) $3 < w < 7$

8 $-11 < m < 8$

9 $-2 < x < 1$

Exercise 4.6 Indices

1 (i) x^4 **(ii)** x^{-8}

(iii) x^1 **(iv)** $x^{\frac{7}{2}}$

(v) x^5 **(vi)** x^9

(vii) x^{10} **(viii)** $x^{-\frac{3}{4}}$

2 (i) $x^5 + x^{-2}$ **(ii)** $2x + 1$

(iii) $1 - 3x^{-3}$ **(iv)** $x - 4x^2$

(v) $3x^2 + 1$

3 (i) $x = \dfrac{1}{7}$ **(ii)** $x = 81$

(iii) $x = \pm 2$ **(iv)** $x = -\dfrac{27}{8}$

(v) $x = \dfrac{1}{2}$ **(vi)** $x = \pm 64$

(vii) $x = \dfrac{1}{16}$ **(viii)** $x = \dfrac{1}{9}$

4 (i) $y = 0$ **(ii)** $x = -2$ or $x = 4$

5 (ii) $x = 2$

6 $x = -1$ or -2

7 $x = 4$ or 9

8 $x = 3$ or ± 2

Exercise 4.7 Algebraic proof

2 (i) $(x - 1)^2 + 2$

8 (i) $\dfrac{x^2 + y^2}{xy}$

Exercise 4.8 Linear sequences

1 (i) $3n + 2$ **(ii)** $4n + 2$

(iii) $10n$ **(iv)** $-5n + 12$

(v) $-3n + 3$ **(vi)** $-4n - 1$

2 (i) 202 **(ii)** 501

(iii) 901 **(iv)** -687

(v) -792 **(vi)** -205

3 (i) 254 **(ii)** 253

(iii) 254 **(iv)** 253

(v) 252 **(vi)** 251

4 (i) -6 **(ii)** -2

(iii) -2 **(iv)** -7

(v) -4 **(vi)** -7

5 (i) $2q - p$

(ii) $(2 - n)p + (n - 1)q$

(iii) $-8p + 9q = 74$

(iv) $p = 11, q = 18$

6 If 654 is in the sequence, then $7n + 2 = 654 \Rightarrow$ $n = 93\dfrac{1}{7}$ but n is an integer, so 654 cannot be in the sequence.

8 $b = \dfrac{a + c}{2}$

Exercise 4.9 Quadratic sequences and the limiting value of a sequence

1 (i) 16 **(ii)** 44

(iii) 38 **(iv)** -5

2 (i) $n^2 + 1$ **(ii)** $n^2 + n + 3$

(iii) $n^2 - n + 1$ **(iv)** $n^2 - n + 3$

(v) $2n^2 - 2n + 5$ **(vi)** $-3n^2 + 8n + 25$

3 (i) 15

(ii) $2n^2 - 3n + 6$

4 (i) $\frac{1}{7}, -\frac{1}{10}, -\frac{3}{13}$

   (ii) $-\frac{2}{3}$

5 (i) −6   **(ii)** −1

6 $3n^2 - n + 1$

7 $-\frac{4}{11}$

8 $p = 6, q = 20$

Exercise 4.10 Simultaneous equations in three unknowns

1 $x = 11, y = 13, z = -12$

2 $x = -1, y = 2, z = 3$

3 (i) $q = -1$

   (ii) $p = 3, r = -3$

4 $x = 1, y = 3, z = -2$

5 $x = 7, y = 2, z = -1$

6 25

7 The first two equations contradict each other.

8 (i) $4a + 2b + c = -4$ $9a + 3b + c = -4$
       $25a + 5b + c = 2$

   (ii) $n^2 - 5n + 2$

5 Coordinate geometry

Exercise 5.1 Parallel and perpendicular lines: distances, midpoints and gradients

1 (i) **(a)** 3   **(c)** $2\sqrt{10}$

      (b) $-\frac{1}{3}$ **(d)** $(3, 4)$

  (ii) **(a)** 2   **(c)** $3\sqrt{5}$

      (b) $-\frac{1}{2}$ **(d)** $(3.5, 6)$

 (iii) **(a)** 0   **(c)** 8

      (b) undefined   **(d)** $(1, 2)$

  (iv) **(a)** 0.2   **(c)** $\sqrt{26}$

      (b) −5   **(d)** $(2.5, 7.5)$

  (v) **(a)** $-\frac{1}{2}$ **(c)** $3\sqrt{5}$

      (b) 2   **(d)** $(1, 4.5)$

  (vi) **(a)** 1   **(c)** $7\sqrt{2}$

      (b) −1   **(d)** $(-1.5, 0.5)$

 (vii) **(a)** $-\frac{4}{9}$ **(c)** $\sqrt{97}$

           (b) $\frac{9}{4}$ **(d)** $(-4.5, 0)$

(viii) **(a)** 1   **(c)** $2\sqrt{2}$

          (b) −1   **(d)** $(5, -5)$

2 (i)

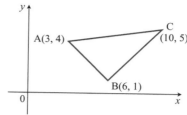

 (iv) 12 units^2

3 (i)

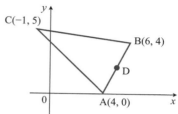

 (iii) 15 units^2

4 (i) $AB = 10, BC = \sqrt{10}, AC = 3\sqrt{10}$,
      right angle at C

  (ii) 15 units^2

5 (i) $x = 7$

  (ii) $AB : BC = 3 : 1$

6 a rectangle

7 (i)

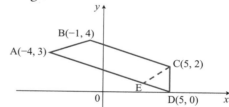

  (ii) a trapezium

 (iii) E is $(2, 1)$

8

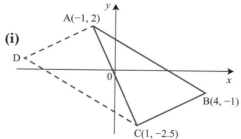

  (ii) $(-4, 0.5)$

9 (i)

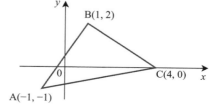

  (ii) right-angled isosceles

10 (i)

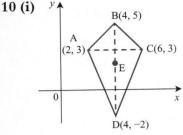

(ii) See full worked solution online.

(iii) 14 units^2

(iv) 6 units^2; 8 units^2

11 (i) See full worked solution online.

(ii) $(-3.5, -0.5)$

(iii) 17.5 units^2

12 (i) See full worked solution online.

(ii) D is $(0, 4)$; 8 units^2

13 (i) midpoint $\left(\dfrac{p+q}{2}, \dfrac{p+q}{2}\right)$

(ii) See full worked solution online.

14 (i)

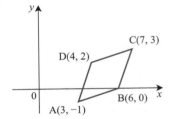

a rhombus

(ii) See full worked solution online.

(iii) $2\sqrt{10}$ units^2

15 $b^2 + ac - bd = 0$

16

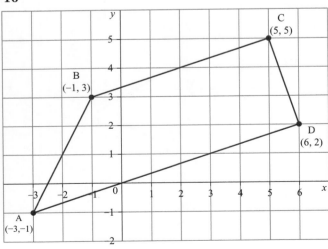

25 units^2

Exercise 5.2 Equations of straight lines

1 (i) perpendicular   **(ii)** parallel

  (iii) neither   **(iv)** neither

  (v) neither   **(vi)** parallel

  (vii) perpendicular   **(viii)** neither

2 (i) $4x + y - 11 = 0$

  (ii) $y = 5x - 7$

  (iii) $4x + y - 17 = 0$

  (iv) $2x - 3y + 14 = 0$ $\left(\text{or } y = \dfrac{2}{3}x + 4\dfrac{2}{3}\right)$

  (v) $x - 2y - 1 = 0$ $\left(\text{or } y = \dfrac{1}{2}x - \dfrac{1}{2}\right)$

  (vi) $2x + 3y - 7 = 0$ $\left(\text{or } y = -\dfrac{2}{3}x + 2\dfrac{1}{3}\right)$

3 (i) $x + 3y - 6 = 0$ $\left(\text{or } y = -\dfrac{1}{3}x + 2\right)$

  (ii) $2y + x - 1 = 0$ $\left(\text{or } y = -\dfrac{1}{2}x + \dfrac{1}{2}\right)$

  (iii) $y = x + 6$

  (iv) $y = \dfrac{3x}{2}$

  (v) $2x + 3y = 0$ $\left(\text{or } y = -\dfrac{2}{3}x\right)$

  (vi) $3x + 4y - 8 = 0$ $\left(\text{or } y = -\dfrac{3}{4}x + 2\right)$

4 (i)

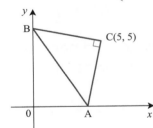

  (ii) A is $(4, 0)$, B is $(0, 6)$

  (iii) 13 units^2

5 (i) $A(-4, 0), B(0, 3)$

  (ii)

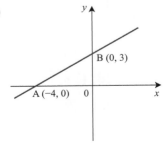

  (iii) 6 units^2

  (iv) $4x + 3y = 0$

  (v) Length of AB $= 5$

Shortest (i.e. perpendicular) distance from
O to AB = 2.4 units

6 (i)

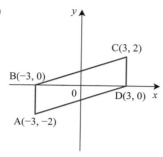

(ii) AB and CD are parallel; gradient

BC = gradient AD = $\frac{1}{3}$; parallelogram.

(iii) 12 units²

(iv) 33.7° (1 d.p.)

7 (i)

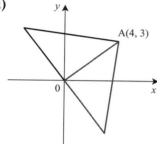

(ii) OA = 5, OB = 5, AB = $5\sqrt{2}$

(iii) Equation of OA is $y = \frac{3}{4}x$

Equation of OB is $y = -\frac{4}{3}x$

Equation of AB is $x + 7y = 25$

(iv) $(3, -4)$

(v) AB is the line of symmetry for the triangle,
so triangle ABC is isosceles.
Area = 25 units²

8 (i)

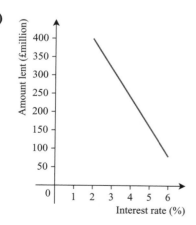

(ii) $y = 640 - 100x$

(iii) (a) £440 million

(b) £140 million

9 (i)

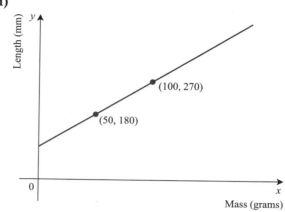

(ii) $y = 1.8x + 90$

(iii) 90 mm

(iv) $83\frac{1}{3}$ g

(v) Adding a load of 1 kg is likely to cause the
elastic band to snap.

10 (i)

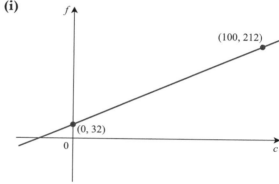

(ii) $f = 1.8c + 32$

(iii) -40

Exercise 5.3 The intersection of two lines

1 (i) $x = 1, y = 2$ **(ii)** $x = 1, y = 1.5$

2 (i) $x = 2, y = -1$ **(ii)** $x = -3, y = 1$

3 (i)

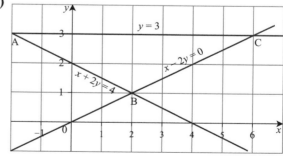

(ii) $y = 3, x + 2y = 4: (-2, 3)$

$y = 3, x - 2y = 0: (6, 3)$

$x + 2y = 4, x - 2y = 0: (2, 1)$

(iii) 8 units²

(iv) Isosceles triangle

4 (i)

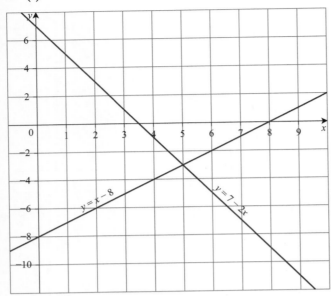

(ii) 6.75 units^2

(iii) 37.5 units^2

5 (i) AB $= 2\sqrt{5}$; BC $= \sqrt{5}$; AC $= 5$

(ii) Gradient AB $= 0.5$; Gradient BC $= -2$; Gradient AC $= 0$

(iii) Triangle is right angled

(iv) 5 units^2

6 (i) D is $(10, 2)$

(ii) AB and AD are perpendicular

(iii) 5616 cm^2

7 Amanda earns £8.50 per day and Belinda earns £10.50 per day.

8 18 10p coins and 30 20p coins.

9 Man is 70 years old and grandson is 10 years old.

10 (i) Individual prices cannot be found from this information, since there are not two 'different' equations – the second is 1.5 times the first. They represent lines that are parallel.

(ii) (a) $x = z + 2, y = 15 - 5z$

(b) $0 = 0$

(c) Each equation will represent a plane and the two planes have no common point – they are parallel.

Exercise 5.4 Dividing of a line in a given ratio

1 (i) C is $(7, 5)$ **(ii)** C is $(-2, 2)$

(iii) C is $(3, 0)$ **(iv)** C is $(-1, -3)$

2 (i) R is $(8, 6.5)$ **(ii)** R is $(12, -2.4)$

(iii) Q is $(4, -1)$ **(iv)** P is $(-6, 5)$

3 (i)

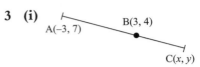

(ii) $\Rightarrow$ AB : BC = 3 : 2

(iii) C is $(7, 2)$

4 (i)

P(–3, 7)   Q   R(6, 1)

(ii) Q is $(0, 5)$

5 (i) $\pi : 1$ **(ii)** $4 : 1$

(iii) $25 : 36$ **(iv)** $25 : 36$

6 Anna receives £44 000
Brian receives £52 000
Charlotte receives £54 000

7 Age 4 receives 80°
Age 6 receives 120°
Age 8 receives 160°

8 (i) Materials $= £75 000$
Wages $= £150 000$
Admin $= £25 000$

(ii) £261 250. Increase $= 4.5\%$

Exercise 5.5 Equation of a circle

1 (i) $x^2 + (y - 1)^2 = 9$

(ii) $(x - 3)^2 + y^2 = 25$

(iii) $(x + 2)^2 + (y - 5)^2 = 4$

(iv) $(x - 4)^2 + (y + 3)^2 = 9$

(v) $(x + 6)^2 + (y + 2)^2 = 16$

2 (i) (a) Centre $(0, 0)$

(b) Radius $= 2$

(c)

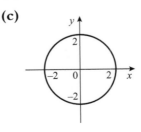

(ii) (a) Centre $(2, 0)$

(b) Radius $= 3$

(c)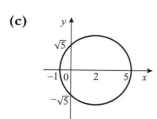

(iii) **(a)** Centre $(0, -3)$

(b) Radius = 3

(c)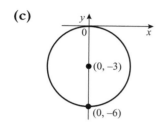

(iv) **(a)** Centre $(5, 5)$

(b) Radius 5

(c)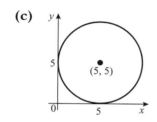

(v) **(a)** Centre $(-3, 4)$

(b) Radius 5

(c)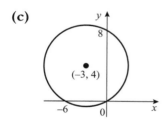

3 **(i)** $(x - 2)^2 + (y - 3)^2 = 4$

(ii) $(x + 1)^2 + (y - 2)^2 = 18$

(iii) $(x - 1)^2 + (y + 1)^2 = 9$

4 Centre $(-2, 3)$, radius 5

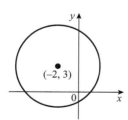

5 $(x + 2)^2 + (y - 3)^2 = -6$; for a circle, RHS must be positive $\Rightarrow$ not a circle

6 $(x - 2)^2 + (y - 7)^2 = 25$

7 **(i)**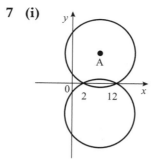

(ii) $(7, 12)$

(iii) $(7, -12)$

(iv) Equation of the top circle is
$(x - 7)^2 + (y - 12)^2 = 169$
Equation of the bottom circle is
$(x - 7)^2 + (y + 12)^2 = 169$

(v) $(0, 1.05)$ and $(0, 22.95)$ (2 d.p.)
$(0, -1.05)$ and $(0, -22.95)$ (2 d.p.)

8 $(x - 3)^2 + (y + 2)^2 = 13$ i.e. a circle
Centre $(3, -2)$, radius $\sqrt{13}$
Concentric circle with radius
5 is $(x - 3)^2 + (y + 2)^2 = 25$

9 **(i)** $(x + 1)^2 + (y - 1)^2 = 25$

(ii) $(x + 1)^2 + (y - 1)^2 = 100$

10 Midpoint C is $(2, 11)$; $(x - 2)^2 + (y - 11)^2 = 10$

11 $(x - 3)^2 + (y - \sqrt{5})^2 = 9$ (top)

Or $(x - 3)^2 + (y + \sqrt{5})^2 = 9$ (bottom)

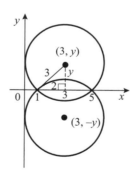

Exercise 5.6 Circle geometry, including tangents and chords

1 Gradient BP $= \dfrac{1}{5} = 0.2$

2 **(i)** $(8, 2)$

(ii) $3\sqrt{5}$

(iii) $5\sqrt{2}$

(iv) $(x - 11)^2 + (y - 8)^2 = 50$

3 (i) Radius = 10; Centre $(2, -3)$

(ii) $y_1 = 5$ and $y_2 = -11$

(iii) 48 units^2

4 (i) Radius = $\sqrt{5}$

(ii) $x - 2y + 1 = 0$

5 (i) $y = 9$

(ii) Tangent at $(-3, 0)$ has equation
$3x + 4y + 9 = 0$
Tangent at $(0, 9)$ has equation $y = 9$
Point of intersection is $(-15, 9)$

6 (i) Radius 5

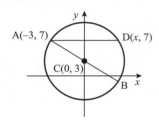

(ii) B is $(3, -1)$; D is $(3, 7)$

(iii) ABD is a right–angled triangle

7 (i) Centre $(1, -2)$; Radius 5

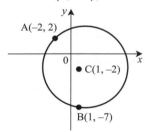

(ii) $3x - 4y + 14 = 0$; $y = -7$

(iii) $(-14, -7)$

8 (i) Centre $(0, -5)$; Radius 5

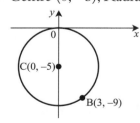

(ii) $3x - 4y - 45 = 0$
A is $(15, 0)$

(iii)

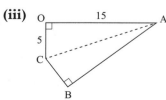

75 units^2

9 (i) $x^2 + y^2 - 6y = 0$

(ii)

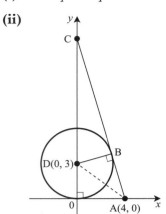

(iii) 12 units^2

6 Geometry I

Exercise 6.1 Circle theorems

1 119°

2 30°

3 27°

4 See full worked solution online.

5 $\angle PQR = 70°$; $\angle PRQ = 70°$; $\angle QPR = 40°$

6 65°

7 $x = 26°$; $y = 122°$

8 (i) $180° - 7x$

(ii) 15°

9 38°

10 (i) $y = 2x - 180°$

(ii) See full worked solution online.

Exercise 6.2 Geometric proof

1 (i) $\angle CAB = \angle CBA = 90° - \dfrac{y}{2}$

$\angle CBD = \angle CDB = 90° - \dfrac{x}{2}$

1(ii), 2–8 See full worked solutions online.

Exercise 6.3 Trigonometry in two dimensions

1 (i) 6.0 cm   **(ii)** 9.5 cm (1 d.p.)

(iii) 7.8 cm (1 d.p.)   **(iv)** 10.2 cm (1 d.p.)

2 (i) 53.3° (1 d.p.)   **(ii)** 53.5° (1 d.p.)

(iii) 33.7° (1 d.p.)   **(iv)** 49.9° (1 d.p.)

3 (i) 79.5° (1 d.p.)   **(ii)** 6.8 cm (1 d.p.)

   (iii) 14.7 cm (1 d.p.) **(iv)** 48.0° (1 d.p.)

4 (i) $\angle ADB = 53.0°$ (1 d.p.)

   (ii) $\angle DCB = 42.4°$ (1 d.p.)

   (iii) 17.9 cm

5 (i)

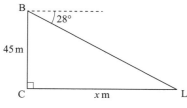

   (ii) $x = 84.6$ m

6 (i)

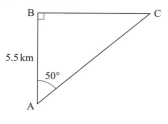

   (ii) 8.55648 … km = 8556 m (nearest metre)

   (iii) 12 055 m

7 (i)

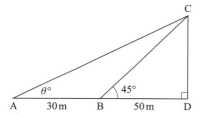

   (ii) 50 m

   (iii) 32.0°

8 (i)

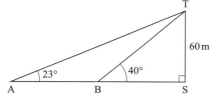

   (ii) 71.5 m

   (iii) 69.8 m

Exercise 6.4 Angles of 45°, 30° and 60°

1 (i) $x = 2\sqrt{3} - 1$

   (ii) $x = 6$

   (iii) $x = 3\sqrt{2}$

   (iv) $x = \dfrac{5}{\sqrt{3}} = \dfrac{5\sqrt{3}}{3}$

2 $AB = \dfrac{2\sqrt{3}}{3}$ cm

   Area $= \dfrac{2\sqrt{3}}{3}$ cm^2

3 $9\sqrt{3}$ cm^2

4 (i) $BD = \sqrt{2}$ cm

   (ii) $DC = \sqrt{6}$ cm

   (iii) Area ABC $= \left(1 + \sqrt{3}\right)$ cm^2

5 (i)

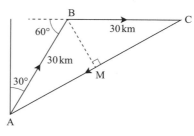

   (ii) $AC = 30\sqrt{3}$ km

   (iii) 3h 44 min

6 (i)

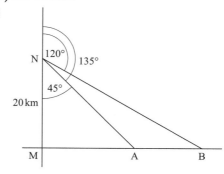

   (ii) $MA = 20$ km

   (iii) $AB = (20\sqrt{3} - 20)$ km

7 (i)

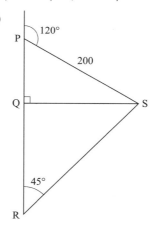

   (ii) $QS = 100\sqrt{3}$ m

      $RS = 100\sqrt{6}$ m

8 (i)

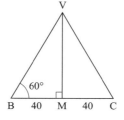

   Area VBC $= 1600\sqrt{3}$ cm^2

   (ii) $6400(\sqrt{3} + 1)$ cm^2

   (iii) $40\sqrt{2}$ cm

Exercise 6.5 Trigonometric functions for angles of any size, and trigonometric graphs

1 (i) $\theta = 30°, 150°$

(ii) $\theta = 30°, 330°$

(iii) $\theta = 63.4°, 243.4°$

(iv) $\theta = 120°, 240°$

(v) $\theta = 125.3°, 305.3°$

(vi) $\theta = 240°, 300°$

2 (i) $\theta = 23.6°, 156.4°$

(ii) $\theta = 63.6°, -63.6°$

(iii) $\theta = 74.1°, -105.9°$

(iv) $\theta = 138.6°, -138.6°$

(v) $\theta = -71.6°, 108.4°$

(vi) $\theta = -23.6°, -156.4°$

3 (i) $\theta = 50.8°, 129.2°, 230.8°, 309.2°$

(ii) $\theta = 50.8°, 129.2°, 230.8°, 309.2°$

(iii) $\theta = 72.5°, 107.5°, 252.5°, 287.5°$

4 (i) $(3x + 2)(x - 1)$

(ii) $x = 1$ or $-\dfrac{2}{3}$

(iii) (a) $\theta = -360°, 0°, 360°$

or $-228.2°, -131.8°, 131.8°, 228.2°$

(b) $\theta = 90°, -270°$

or $-41.8°, -138.2°, 221.8°, 318.2°$

(c) $\theta = 45°, 225°, -135°, -315°$

or $-33.7°, -213.7°, 146.3°, 326.3°$

5 (i) $\theta = -90°, 30°, 150°$

(ii) $\theta = -111.8°, -45°, 68.2°, 135°$

(iii) $\theta = -120°, -41.4°, 41.4°, 120°$

(iv) $\theta = -138.2°, -41.8°, 41.8°, 138.2°$

6 $\theta = 90°, 210°, 330°$

7 (i) $\theta = -360°, 0°, 360°$

(ii) $\theta = -315°, -45°, 45°, 315°$

(iii) $\theta = -300°, -60°, 60°, 300°$

(iv) $\theta = -270°, 90°$

(v) $\theta = -315°, -225°, 45°, 135°$

(vi) $\theta = -330°, -210°, 30°, 150°$

(vii) $\theta = -315°, -135°, 45°, 225°$

(viii) $\theta = -330°, -150°, 30°, 210°$

(ix) $\theta = -300°, -120°, 60°, 240°$

8 (i) $f(\frac{1}{2}) = 0$

(ii) $\theta = -180°, -120°, -60°, 60°, 120°, 180°$

Exercise 6.6 Trigonometric identities

1 (i) (a) $-\cos^2\theta = 0$

(b) $\theta = 90°$

(ii) (a) $\cos^2\theta = 1$

(b) $\theta = 0°, 180°$

(iii) (a) $2\sin^2\theta - \sin\theta - 1 = 0$

(b) $\theta = 90°$

(iv) (a) $2\cos^2\theta - \cos\theta - 1 = 0$

(b) $\theta = 0°, 120°$

(v) (a) $\sin^2\theta - \sin\theta = 0$

(b) $\theta = 0°, 90°, 180°$

(vi) (a) $\cos^2\theta - \cos\theta = 0$

(b) $\theta = 0°, 90°$

2 (i) (a) $\cos^2\theta - \cos\theta - 1 = 0$

(b) $\theta = 128.2°$

(ii) (a) $\sin^2\theta - \sin\theta - 1 = 0$

(b) No soln in interval $0 \leqslant \theta \leqslant 180°$

(iii) (a) $2\cos^2\theta - \cos\theta - 2 = 0$

(b) $\theta = 141.3°$

(iv) (a) $4\cos^2\theta + 5\cos\theta - 6 = 0$

(b) $\theta = 41.4°$

3 (i) $\tan\theta = \dfrac{1}{4}$

(ii) $\theta = 14.0°$

4 (i) $54.7°, 125.3°, 234.7°, 305.3°$

(ii) $116.6°, 296.6°$

(iii) $123.7°, 303.7°$

(iv) $68.2°, 248.2°$

5 (i) $\cos\theta - \cos^3\theta$

(ii) $\dfrac{(1-\cos^2\theta)(2\cos\theta-1)}{\cos\theta}$

6 $\tan^2 x$

7 (i) See full worked solution online.

(ii) See full worked solution online.

8 (i) $\dfrac{2}{\sin^2 x}$

(ii) $x = 45°, 135°, 225°, 315°$

9 $x = 60°, 109.5°, 250.5°, 300°$

7 Geometry II

Exercise 7.1 The area of a triangle

1 (i) $800.7\,\text{cm}^2$ **(ii)** $1.9\,\text{cm}^2$

2 (i) 14.0   **(ii)** 12.3   **(iii)** 13.0

3 $35.1\,\text{cm}^2$

4 $7.3\,\text{cm}$

5 (i) $35.2°$ or $144.8°$

(ii) $56.1°$ or $33.9°$

6 4.9

7 1.2

8 3.7 or 1.0

9 $2.8\,\text{cm}$

10 $81.1\,\text{m}^2$

11 $17.9°$ and $162.1°$

Exercise 7.2 The sine rule

1 (i) $13.4\,\text{cm}$ **(ii)** $7.1\,\text{cm}$

2 (i) $11.3\,\text{cm}$ **(ii)** $36.8\,\text{cm}$

3 (i) $31.9°$ **(ii)** $35.7°$

4 (i) $43.5°$ or $136.5°$ **(ii)** $6.5°$

5 (i) $7.9\,\text{cm}$ **(ii)** $26.0\,\text{cm}^2$

6 (i) $45.8°$ **(ii)** $77.4\,\text{cm}^2$

7 $\dfrac{4}{11}\sqrt{3}$

8 $46.0\,\text{cm}^2$

9 $53.7\,\text{cm}^2$

Exercise 7.3 The cosine rule

1 (i) $9.1\,\text{cm}$ **(ii)** $12.8\,\text{m}$

2 (i) $77.6°$ **(ii)** $135.8°$

3 (i) $75.0°$ **(ii)** $42.0°$

4 (i) $7.6\,\text{cm}$ **(ii)** $26.0\,\text{cm}^2$

5 (ii) $40.7\,\text{m}^2$ or $11.7\,\text{m}^2$

6 (i) $11.5\,\text{cm}$ **(ii)** $8.0\,\text{cm}$ **(iii)** $46.0\,\text{cm}^2$

7 $9.2\,\text{km}$

8 $\dfrac{120\sqrt{3}-206}{191}$

Exercise 7.4 Using the sine and cosine rules together

1 (i) $13.1\,\text{cm}$ **(ii)** $52.4°$ **(iii)** $72.7\,\text{cm}^2$

2 (i) $11.0\,\text{cm}$ **(ii)** $9.4\,\text{cm}$ **(iii)** $42.1\,\text{cm}^2$

3 $29.2\,\text{cm}^2$

4 (i) $9.3\,\text{km}$ **(ii)** $092.2°$

5 (i) $8.0\,\text{cm}$ **(ii)** $37.3\,\text{cm}^2$

6 $7.2\,\text{cm}$

7 (i) $29.3\,\text{cm}^2$ **(ii)** $7.1\,\text{cm}$

8 (i) $80.0\,\text{cm}^2$ **(ii)** $15.0\,\text{m}$

Exercise 7.5 Problems in three dimensions

1 (i) $12.4\,\text{cm}$ **(ii)** $13\,\text{cm}$ **(iii)** $17.9°$

2 (i) $26.2°$ **(ii)** $69.9°$ **(iii)** $78.6\,\text{cm}^2$

3 (i) $6.9\,\text{cm}$ **(iii)** $63.1°$

(ii) $59.7°$ **(iv)** $32.3°$

4 $49.1°$

5 (i) $86.6\,\text{cm}^2$ **(ii)** $54.7°$

6 (i) $15\,\text{cm}$ **(iii)** $13\,\text{cm}$

(ii) $18.4°$ **(iv)** $34.7°$

7 (i) $3.2\,\text{cm}$ **(ii)** $115.8\,\text{cm}^3$ **(iii)** 492

8 (i) $61.9°$ **(ii)** $69.3°$

9 (i) $14.1\,\text{cm}$ **(iii)** $20.3\,\text{cm}$

(ii) $21.2\,\text{cm}$ **(iv)** $80.0°$

10 (i) $26.6°$ **(ii)** $20\,\text{m}^3$ **(iii)** $5.1\,\text{m}$

11 (i) 25.9 m **(ii)** 297.0 m

12 (i) 27.0 m **(iii)** 93.2° **(v)** 437.5 m³

  (ii) 3.4° **(iv)** 12.0 m

13 (i) 3.1 m; 3.7 m **(ii)** 14.8°, 17.6°

14 (i) 914.4 m from A, 761.1 m from B

  (ii) 534.4 m

  (iii) 8.5°

8 Calculus

Exercise 8.1 Differentiation

1 (i) $\dfrac{dy}{dx} = 12x^2$ **(ii)** $\dfrac{dy}{dx} = 6x$

  (iii) $\dfrac{dy}{dx} = 4$ **(iv)** $\dfrac{dy}{dx} = -42x^6$

  (v) $\dfrac{dy}{dx} = -42x^5$ **(vi)** $\dfrac{dy}{dx} = 0$

  (vii) $\dfrac{dy}{dx} = x$ **(viii)** $\dfrac{dy}{dx} = x^2$

  (ix) $\dfrac{dy}{dx} = x^3$

2 (i) $\dfrac{dy}{dx} = 6x^2 + 6x$ **(ii)** $\dfrac{dy}{dx} = 12x^3 + 12x^2$

  (iii) $\dfrac{dy}{dx} = 20x^4 + 20x^3$ **(iv)** $\dfrac{dy}{dx} = 3$

  (v) $\dfrac{dy}{dx} = 2$ **(vi)** $\dfrac{dy}{dx} = -4$

  (vii) $\dfrac{dy}{dx} = 9x^2$ **(viii)** $\dfrac{dy}{dx} = 16x^3$

  (ix) $\dfrac{dy}{dx} = 25x^4$

3 (i) $\dfrac{dy}{dx} = 8x^3 - 8x - 8$

  (ii) $\dfrac{dy}{dx} = 12x^3 - 12x^2 + 12$

  (iii) $\dfrac{dy}{dx} = 10x^4 + 10x - 10$

4 (i) $\dfrac{dy}{dx} = 1 + 2x^{-2} = 1 + \dfrac{2}{x^2}$

  (ii) $\dfrac{dy}{dx} = \dfrac{2x}{2} + 4x^{-3} = x + \dfrac{4}{x^3}$

  (iii) $\dfrac{dy}{dx} = \dfrac{3x^2}{3} + 9x^{-4} = x^2 + \dfrac{9}{x^4}$

  (iv) $\dfrac{dy}{dx} = 3x^2 + 3x^{-4} = 3x^2 + \dfrac{3}{x^4}$

  (v) $\dfrac{dy}{dx} = 8x^3 + 8x^{-3} = 8x^3 + \dfrac{8}{x^3}$

  (vi) $\dfrac{dy}{dx} = 20x^4 - 20x^{-5} = 20x^4 - \dfrac{20}{x^5}$

5 (i) $\dfrac{dy}{dx} = 12x^2 + 12x^{-5} = 12x^2 + \dfrac{12}{x^5}$

  (ii) $\dfrac{dy}{dx} = 1 + 1x^{-2} = 1 + \dfrac{1}{x^2}$

  (iii) $\dfrac{dy}{dx} = 4x + \dfrac{1}{2}x^{-2} = 4x + \dfrac{1}{2x^2}$

  (iv) $\dfrac{dy}{dx} = -6x^{-3} - 6x^{-4} = -\dfrac{6}{x^3} - \dfrac{6}{x^4}$

  (v) $\dfrac{dy}{dx} = -\dfrac{4}{5}x^{-3} + \dfrac{25}{2}x^{-6} = \dfrac{-4}{5x^3} + \dfrac{25}{2x^6}$

  (vi) $y = -12x^{-4} + 12x^{-5} = \dfrac{-12}{x^4} + \dfrac{12}{x^5}$

6 (i) $V = 24x^3$

  $A = 52x^2$

  (ii) $\dfrac{dV}{dx} = 72x^2$

  $\dfrac{dA}{dx} = 104x$

7 (i) At $(1, 0)$ $\dfrac{dy}{dx} = -2$

  At $(3, 0)$ $\dfrac{dy}{dx} = 2$

  (ii) At $(0, 3)$ $\dfrac{dy}{dx} = -4$

8 $(-2, 11), (1, -16)$

Exercise 8.2 Gradient functions and more complex differentiation

1 (i) $\dfrac{dy}{dx} = 6x^2 - 6x$

  (ii) $\dfrac{dy}{dx} = 18x^2 - 15$

  (iii) $\dfrac{dy}{dx} = 2x + 3$

  (iv) $\dfrac{dy}{dx} = 2x - 1$

  (v) $\dfrac{dy}{dx} = 12x + 1$

  (vi) $\dfrac{dy}{dx} = 18x^2 + 30x - 4$

2 (i) $2x^3 - 6x^2 + 5x - 15$

  (ii) $\dfrac{dy}{dx} = 6x^2 - 12x + 5$

  (iii) She has not multiplied out the brackets before differentiating.

3 (i) $4x^2 + 2$ **(ii)** $\dfrac{dy}{dx} = 8x$

4 (i) $\dfrac{dy}{dx} = \dfrac{4x}{5} + \dfrac{3}{5}$

(ii) $\dfrac{dy}{dx} = 2x - 2$

(iii) $\dfrac{dy}{dx} = 4 - 6x$

(iv) $\dfrac{dy}{dx} = 5x^4 + \dfrac{8}{3}x^3 - 3x^2$

(v) $\dfrac{dy}{dx} = 6x + 12x^2$

(vi) $\dfrac{dy}{dx} = 4x - 2$

5 (i) 0   **(ii)** 8   **(iii)** 20

6 (i) 1   **(ii)** −2   **(iii)** 94

7 (i) 79   **(ii)** −6   **(iii)** 9

8 $\dfrac{dy}{dx} = 8$

9 2

10 $(-2, 54)$ and $(3, -71)$

11 Gradients at intersection with the x-axis are 18, −9, 18

Gradient at intersection with the y-axis is −6

Exercise 8.3 Tangents and normal

1 (i) $2x$

(ii) 2

(iii) $y = 2x - 5$

(iv) $x + 2y + 5 = 0$

2 (i) $3x^2 - 4x - 5$

(ii) −6 at $(1, 0)$

15 at $(-2, 0)$

10 at $(3, 0)$

(iii) $x + y + 2 = 0$

(iv) $y = x - 6$

3 (i)

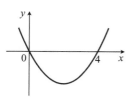

(ii) $\dfrac{dy}{dx} = 6$

4 (i) $3x^2 - 12x + 11$

(ii) See full worked solution online.

5 (i) $x = 1 \Rightarrow \dfrac{dy}{dx} = 2$

$x = -1 \Rightarrow \dfrac{dy}{dx} = -2$

(ii) $x = 1 \Rightarrow \dfrac{dy}{dx} = -2$

$x = -1 \Rightarrow \dfrac{dy}{dx} = 2$

(iii) $y = 2x - 5$

$y = -2x - 5$

$y = -2x + 5$

$y = 2x + 5$

(iv)

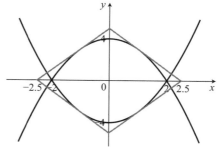

$(-2.5, 0)$ and $(2.5, 0)$

(v) a rhombus

6 (i)

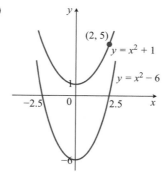

(ii) $\dfrac{dy}{dx} = 4$

(iii) Using geometry, $y = x^2 + 1$ is the same shape as $y = x^2 - 6$ but moved vertically up through 7 units.

Using calculus, $y = x^2 - 6 \Rightarrow \dfrac{dy}{dx} = 2x$

At $(2, -2)$, $\dfrac{dy}{dx} = 4$

(iv) Any curve of the form $y = x^2 + c$, where c is constant.

7 (i) $8a + 8 + b = 0$

(ii) $f'(x) = 3ax^2 + 4x$

$-4 = 12a + 8$

(iii) $a = -1, b = 0$

(iv)

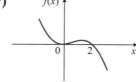

8 (i) Replacing x by $(-x)$ gives the same value of $y \Rightarrow$ symmetrical about the y-axis.

(ii) $\dfrac{dy}{dx} = 4x^3 - \dfrac{4}{x^3}$

Min turning points are $(-1, 3)$ and $(1, 3)$

(iii) At $(-1, 3)$ tangent is $y = 3$, normal is $x = -1$

At $(1, 3)$ tangent is $y = 3$, normal is $x = 1$

(iv) tangent: $y = 31.5x - 46.5$

normal: $2x + 63y = 1043.5$

(v) tangent: $y = -31.5x - 46.5$

normal: $2x - 63y = 1043.5$

Exercise 8.4 Increasing and decreasing functions

1 (i) Increasing for $x > 0$

(ii) Increasing for all x

(iii) Increasing for $x > 2$

(iv) Increasing for $x > -2.5$

(v) Increasing for $x > 1$

(vi) Increasing for $x > 1$

(vii) Increasing for $x < 0$ or $x > 1$

(viii) Increasing for $x < -\dfrac{\sqrt{6}}{3}$ or $x > \dfrac{\sqrt{6}}{3}$

2 (i) Decreasing for $x < 0$

(ii) Decreasing for $x < 2$

(iii) Decreasing for $x < 2$

(iv) Decreasing for $x > \dfrac{1}{4}$

(v) Decreasing for $x < -\dfrac{1}{2}$

(vi) Decreasing for all x

(vii) Decreasing for $x < 1.5$

(viii) Decreasing for $x < -1$ or $x > 1$

3 See full worked solution online.

4 See full worked solution online.

5 (i) (a) Increasing if $x < -\dfrac{1}{2}$ or $x > \dfrac{1}{2}$

(b) Decreasing if $-\dfrac{1}{2} < x < \dfrac{1}{2}$ with $x \neq 0$ (not defined)

(ii) (a) Increasing if $x < -2$ or $x > 3$

(b) Decreasing if $-2 < x < 3$

(iii) (a) Increasing if $x < -\dfrac{1}{\sqrt{3}}$ or $x > \dfrac{1}{\sqrt{3}}$

(b) Decreasing if $-\dfrac{1}{\sqrt{3}} < x < \dfrac{1}{\sqrt{3}}$

(iv) (a) Increasing if $x > 0$

(b) Decreasing if $x < 0$

6 See full worked solution online.

7 (i) Decreasing for $3 < x < 7$

(ii) Increasing for $x < 3$ or $x > 7$

8 (i) $P = 1000$

(ii) $4 + 2t$

(iii) 6%

9 (i) 9134

(ii) 253 per annum

(iii) 2027

Exercise 8.5 Second derivatives

1 (i) $\dfrac{dy}{dx} = 6x^2 - 6x \qquad \dfrac{d^2y}{dx^2} = 12x - 6$

(ii) $\dfrac{dy}{dx} = 5 \qquad \dfrac{d^2y}{dx^2} = 0$

(iii) $\dfrac{dy}{dx} = 4 - 4x^3 \qquad \dfrac{d^2y}{dx^2} = -12x^2$

2 (i) $\dfrac{dy}{dx} = 8x^3 - 6x - 5, \qquad \dfrac{d^2y}{dx^2} = 24x^2 - 6$

(ii) $\dfrac{dy}{dx} = 6x^5 - 12x + 3, \qquad \dfrac{d^2y}{dx^2} = 30x^4 - 12$

(iii) $\dfrac{dy}{dx} = 8x^2 + 8x - 7, \qquad \dfrac{d^2y}{dx^2} = 16x + 8$

3 (i) $\dfrac{dy}{dx} = 12x - 13, \qquad \dfrac{d^2y}{dx^2} = 12$

(ii) $\dfrac{dy}{dx} = 3x^2 + 2x - 1, \qquad \dfrac{d^2y}{dx^2} = 6x + 2$

(iii) $\dfrac{dy}{dx} = 192x^2 - 288x + 108$

$\dfrac{d^2y}{dx^2} = 384x - 288$

4 (i) $\dfrac{dy}{dx} = 60x^2 - 10x + 40, \dfrac{d^2y}{dx^2} = 120x - 10$

(ii) $\dfrac{dy}{dx} = 36x^2 - 24x - 45, \dfrac{d^2y}{dx^2} = 72x - 24$

(iii) $\dfrac{dy}{dx} = 135x^2 - 120x + 20$

$\dfrac{d^2y}{dx^2} = 270x - 120$

5 (i) $y = 20 - x$

(ii) $P = 20x - x^2$

(iii) $\dfrac{dy}{dx} = -1, \qquad \dfrac{dP}{dx} = 20 - 2x$

(iv) $\dfrac{d^2P}{dx^2} = -2$

6 (i) $\dfrac{dy}{dx} = 6x^2 - 6x - 13$, $\quad \dfrac{d^2y}{dx^2} = 12x - 6$

(ii) At $(-2, 10) = 23$ positive so /
At $(0, 12) = -13$ negative so \
At $(3, 0) = 23$ positive so /

(iii)

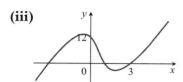

7 (i) $\dfrac{dh}{dt} = 15 - 10t$ $\dfrac{d^2h}{dt^2} = -10$

(ii) When $\dfrac{dh}{dt} = 0$, stone is instantaneously at rest at its highest point.

(iii)

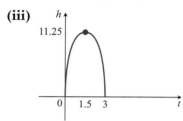

8 (i) At $(-3, 0) = -54$
At $(0, 0) = 0$
At $(3, 0) = 54$

(ii)

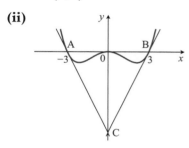

(iii) AB is $y = 0$
AC is $y = -54x - 162$
BC is $y = 54x - 162$
$A(-3, 0), B(3, 0), C(0, -162)$

(iv) 486 units²

Exercise 8.6 Stationary points and applications of maxima and minima

1 (i) (a) $\dfrac{dy}{dx} = 2x - 1$ $\dfrac{dy}{dx} = 0$ when $x = 0.5$

(b) and (c) $\dfrac{d^2y}{dx^2} = 2$ $\Rightarrow$ min turning point

(d) $x = 0.5 \Rightarrow y = -2.25$

(e)

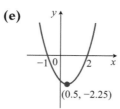

(ii) (a) $\dfrac{dy}{dx} = -5 - 12x$ $\dfrac{dy}{dx} = 0$ when $x = \dfrac{-5}{12}$

(b) and (c) $\dfrac{d^2y}{dx^2} = -12$
$\Rightarrow$ max turning point

(d) $x = \dfrac{-5}{12} \Rightarrow y = 7\dfrac{1}{24}$

(e)

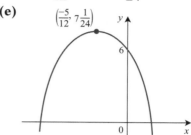

(iii) (a) $\dfrac{dy}{dx} = 3x^2 - 3 = 0$ for $x \pm 1$

(b) $+6$ for $x = 1$
-6 for $x = -1$

(c) max at $x = -1$, min at $x = 1$

(d) $x = -1 \Rightarrow y = 2$
$x = 1 \Rightarrow y = -2$

(e)

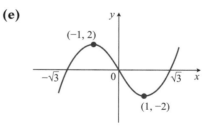

(iv) (a) $\dfrac{dy}{dx} = 3x^2 + 6x - 24$
$x = -4, x = 2$

(b) At $x = -4$ $\dfrac{d^2y}{dx^2} = -18$

At $x = 2$ $\dfrac{d^2y}{dx^2} = 18$

(c) $x = -4 \Rightarrow$ max turning point.
$x = 2 \Rightarrow$ min turning point.

(d) $x = -4 \Rightarrow y = 73$ $x = 2 \Rightarrow y = -35$

(e)

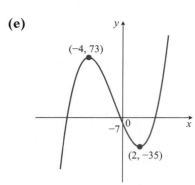

(v) (a) $\dfrac{dy}{dx} = 4x^3 - 4x$

$x = -1$ or $x = 0$ or $x = 1$

(b) At $x = -1 \Rightarrow \dfrac{d^2y}{dx^2} = 8$

At $x = 0 \Rightarrow \dfrac{d^2y}{dx^2} = -4$

At $x = 1 \Rightarrow \dfrac{d^2y}{dx^2} = 8$

(c) $x = -1 \Rightarrow$ min turning point

$x = 0 \Rightarrow$ max turning point

$x = 1 \Rightarrow$ min turning point

(d) $x = -1 \Rightarrow y = 0$ $x = 0 \Rightarrow y = 1$

$x = 1 \Rightarrow y = 0$

(e)

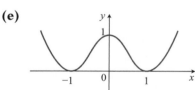

2 $a = 4$, $b = 1$

3 (i) $\dfrac{dy}{dx} = 4x^3 - 16x$, $\dfrac{d^2y}{dx^2} = 12x^2 - 16$

(ii) $x = 0$, $\dfrac{d^2y}{dx^2} = -16 \Rightarrow$ max $(0, 0)$

$x = -2$, $\dfrac{d^2y}{dx^2} = 32 \Rightarrow$ min $(-2, -16)$

$x = 2$, $\dfrac{d^2y}{dx^2} = 32 \Rightarrow$ min $(2, -16)$

(iii)

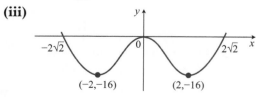

4 (i) $\dfrac{dy}{dx} = 12x^2 - 16$, $\dfrac{d^2y}{dx^2} = 24x$

(ii) min at $\left(\dfrac{2\sqrt{3}}{3}, -\dfrac{64\sqrt{3}}{9} \right)$

max at $\left(\dfrac{-2\sqrt{3}}{3}, \dfrac{64\sqrt{3}}{9} \right)$

(iii)

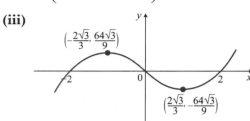

5 (i) $\dfrac{dy}{dx} = 3x^2 - 12x + 9$, $\dfrac{d^2y}{dx^2} = 6x - 12$

(ii) max at $(1, 0)$

min at $(3, -4)$

(iii)

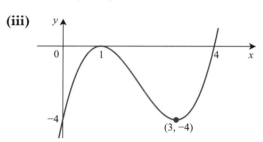

6 (i) $y = 3 + 2x - x^2$

(ii) See full worked solution online.

7 (i) $y = 12 - x$

(ii) $S = 2x^2 - 24x + 144$

(iii) $\dfrac{dS}{dx} = 4x - 24$ $\dfrac{d^2S}{dx^2} = 4$

(iv) $S = x^2 + y^2 = 72$

8 (i) $h = \dfrac{250 - r^2}{2r}$

(ii) $V = \pi r \left(125 - \dfrac{r^2}{2} \right)$

(iii) $\dfrac{dV}{dr} = 125\pi - \dfrac{3\pi r^2}{2}$

$\dfrac{d^2V}{dr^2} = -3\pi r$

(iv) $r = \dfrac{5\sqrt{30}}{3}$ cm, $h = \dfrac{5\sqrt{30}}{3}$ cm

9 (i) $V = 4x^3 - 192x^2 + 2304x$

(ii) $8192 \, cm^2$

10 (i) each side is $(14 - 2x)$ cm
Area $= (196 - 56x + 4x^2) \, cm^2$

(ii) See full worked solution online.

(iii) min A when $x = 4$

(iv) $84 \, cm^2$

Answers

11 (i) $V = 4x^3 - 390x^2 + 9000x$

(ii) $x = 15$

(iii) $60\,750\,\text{cm}^3$

9 Matrices

Exercise 9.1 Multiplying matrices

1 (i) $\begin{bmatrix} -1 & -7 \\ 5 & 14 \end{bmatrix}$ **(ii)** $\begin{bmatrix} -19 & -20 \\ 7 & 23 \end{bmatrix}$

(iii) $\begin{bmatrix} -11 & 11 \\ 12 & 15 \end{bmatrix}$ **(iv)** $\begin{bmatrix} 1 & -18 \\ 6 & 13 \end{bmatrix}$

2 (i) $p = 5.5, q = 29$

(ii) $m = -\dfrac{14}{3}, n = -\dfrac{19}{12}$

3 $m = 24, n = 3, r = 6, t = -3$

4 (i) $a = 1.5$

(ii) $b = 2$

5 (i) $3x + y = 13$ and $2x - 4y = 18$

(ii) $x = 5, y = -2$

6 (i) $w = -110, x = 2, y = -12$

(ii) $p = -\dfrac{13}{3}, \quad q = \dfrac{18}{13}, \quad r = -\dfrac{120}{13}$

7 3

8 (i) $p(p-1) + 2p - q = 10$ and
$4p + 1 = 3p + 2q$ and $p(p-q) + 5q = 13$

(ii) $p = 3$ and $q = 2$

9 $m = -2$ and $n = 6$

10 $b = \dfrac{1}{3}(8 - 2a)$ and $c = 4 - a$

11 (i) $\begin{bmatrix} 14 & -2 \\ 35 & -3 \end{bmatrix}$

(ii) $\begin{bmatrix} -33 & 36 \\ 16 & 8 \end{bmatrix}$

(iii) See full worked solution online.

12 $a = 2, b = -3, c = -1, d = 2$

13 $\begin{bmatrix} -2 & 3 \\ 3 & -4 \end{bmatrix}$

Exercise 9.2 Transformations and matrices

1 (i) $(36, 22)$ **(ii)** $(20, 22)$

2 $(2b - 4a, 3a + b)$

3 (i) -4 **(ii)** $\dfrac{1}{3}$ **(iii)** 1

4 (i) $a + 2b = 3$ and $2a - 2b = 4$

(ii) $a = \dfrac{7}{3}$ and $b = \dfrac{1}{3}$

5 (i) $\begin{bmatrix} -2 & -7 \\ -2 & 6 \end{bmatrix}$

(ii) $\begin{bmatrix} 8 & -3 \\ 1 & 2 \end{bmatrix}$

(iii) $\begin{bmatrix} 4 & 0 \\ 2 & 2 \end{bmatrix}$

6 $\begin{bmatrix} 3 & -1 \\ 3 & 5 \end{bmatrix}$

7 (i) $c = 7$ **(ii)** $d = 4, e = 5$

8 (i) $(1, 2)$ **(ii)** $(32, -14)$

9 See full worked solution online.

10 (i) $x + 3y = 0$ or any equivalent equation

(ii) e.g. $(3, -1)$

Exercise 9.3 Transformations of the unit square

1 (i) $\begin{bmatrix} -1 & 0 \\ 0 & 1 \end{bmatrix}$ **(ii)** $\begin{bmatrix} 1 & 0 \\ 0 & -1 \end{bmatrix}$

(iii) $\begin{bmatrix} 0 & 1 \\ 1 & 0 \end{bmatrix}$ **(iv)** $\begin{bmatrix} 0 & -1 \\ -1 & 0 \end{bmatrix}$

2 (i) $\begin{bmatrix} 0 & -1 \\ 1 & 0 \end{bmatrix}$ **(ii)** $\begin{bmatrix} 0 & 1 \\ -1 & 0 \end{bmatrix}$

(iii) $\begin{bmatrix} -1 & 0 \\ 0 & -1 \end{bmatrix}$

3 (i) $\begin{bmatrix} 7 & 0 \\ 0 & 7 \end{bmatrix}$ **(ii)** $\begin{bmatrix} \dfrac{1}{3} & 0 \\ 0 & \dfrac{1}{3} \end{bmatrix}$

(iii) $\begin{bmatrix} -4 & 0 \\ 0 & -4 \end{bmatrix}$

4 (i) enlargement, scale factor 3, centre $(0, 0)$

(ii) reflection in the line $y = x$

(iii) rotation of 90° about $(0, 0)$

(iv) rotation of 180° about $(0, 0)$

(v) rotation of 270° about $(0, 0)$

(vi) reflection in the y-axis

5 (i) $\begin{bmatrix} 0 & -1 \\ 1 & 0 \end{bmatrix}$ (ii) $\begin{bmatrix} 0 & 1 \\ -1 & 0 \end{bmatrix}$

(iii) $\begin{bmatrix} 0 & -1 \\ -1 & 0 \end{bmatrix}$ (iv) $\begin{bmatrix} 2 & 0 \\ 0 & 2 \end{bmatrix}$

6 36

7 a^2

8 (i) $P' = (a, c), Q' = (a + b, c + d), R' = (b, d)$

(ii) $\begin{pmatrix} b \\ d \end{pmatrix}$ (iii) See full worked solution online.

Exercise 9.4 Combining transformations

1 (i) $\begin{bmatrix} 2 & -2 \\ -1 & 3 \end{bmatrix}$ (ii) $(-4, 8)$

2 (i) $\begin{bmatrix} 0 & 1 \\ 1 & 0 \end{bmatrix}$ (ii) $\begin{bmatrix} 1 & 0 \\ 0 & -1 \end{bmatrix}$

(iii) $\begin{bmatrix} 0 & 1 \\ -1 & 0 \end{bmatrix}$

(iv) rotation of 270° about $(0, 0)$

3 (i) $\begin{bmatrix} 0 & -1 \\ -1 & 0 \end{bmatrix}$ (ii) $(2, -4)$

4 (i) $\begin{bmatrix} -7 & 0 \\ 0 & -7 \end{bmatrix}$ (ii) $\begin{bmatrix} 0 & -1 \\ -1 & 0 \end{bmatrix}$

(iii) $\begin{bmatrix} 0 & 7 \\ 7 & 0 \end{bmatrix}$ (iv) 49

5 (i) $\begin{bmatrix} -111 & 171 \\ 2 & -18 \end{bmatrix}$

(ii) $(-393, 22)$

6 (i) $\begin{bmatrix} -10 & -10 \\ 52 & 91 \end{bmatrix}$ (ii) $(2, 3)$

7 See full worked solution online.

8 $\begin{bmatrix} -1 & 0 \\ 0 & -1 \end{bmatrix}$

9 $\begin{bmatrix} \dfrac{1}{k} & 0 \\ 0 & \dfrac{1}{k} \end{bmatrix}$

10 $\begin{bmatrix} 1 & 0 \\ 0 & 1 \end{bmatrix}$